AF575184

Acknowledgments

The Arkansas Arts Center Foundation Board of Directors

On a Clear Day

The Paintings of George Dombek

1975 - 1994

Introduction and Book Narrative by Donald Harington

Foreword by Townsend Wolfe
and Ruth Pasquine

Copyright

On a Clear Day

The Paintings of George Dombek

Foreword by Townsend Wolfe and Ruth Pasquine
Introduction and Book Narrative by Donald Harington
Book design by Pat Cross
Printed and bound by Sung In Printing Co., Ltd., Seoul, Korea.

Published by the University of Central Arkansas Press
Conway, AR

ISBN 0-944436-17-X
Printed in Korea

Special Thanks

The most enjoyable aspect of working on this book is the opportunity to publicly thank the people who have supported and encouraged me as a painter. Without the teachers, friends and patrons, the path would have been much more difficult.

I want to thank my wife, Karen Vanderveen, for her continuous support and good humor. Without Bob Lowrey and the University of Central Arkansas Press Committee, and Townsend Wolfe, Ruth Pasquine and the staff of the Arkansas Arts Center, this book and the exhibit would never have happened. Special thanks go to Donald Harington for his insight and patience.

I'm grateful to the many people who worked on this project including Pat Cross, Rhonda Hammond, Stewart Nelson, Gregory Register and Mickey Adair.

For many years I've owed gratitude to Tom Porter, Coy Cornelius, Hugh Harris, Peggy Harper, Robert Ross, Neppie Conner, and Elam Denham.

I would also like to thank Dean Roy Knight and my colleagues at the Florida A&M University School of Architecture.

And finally, much love and appreciation goes to my family.

george dombek

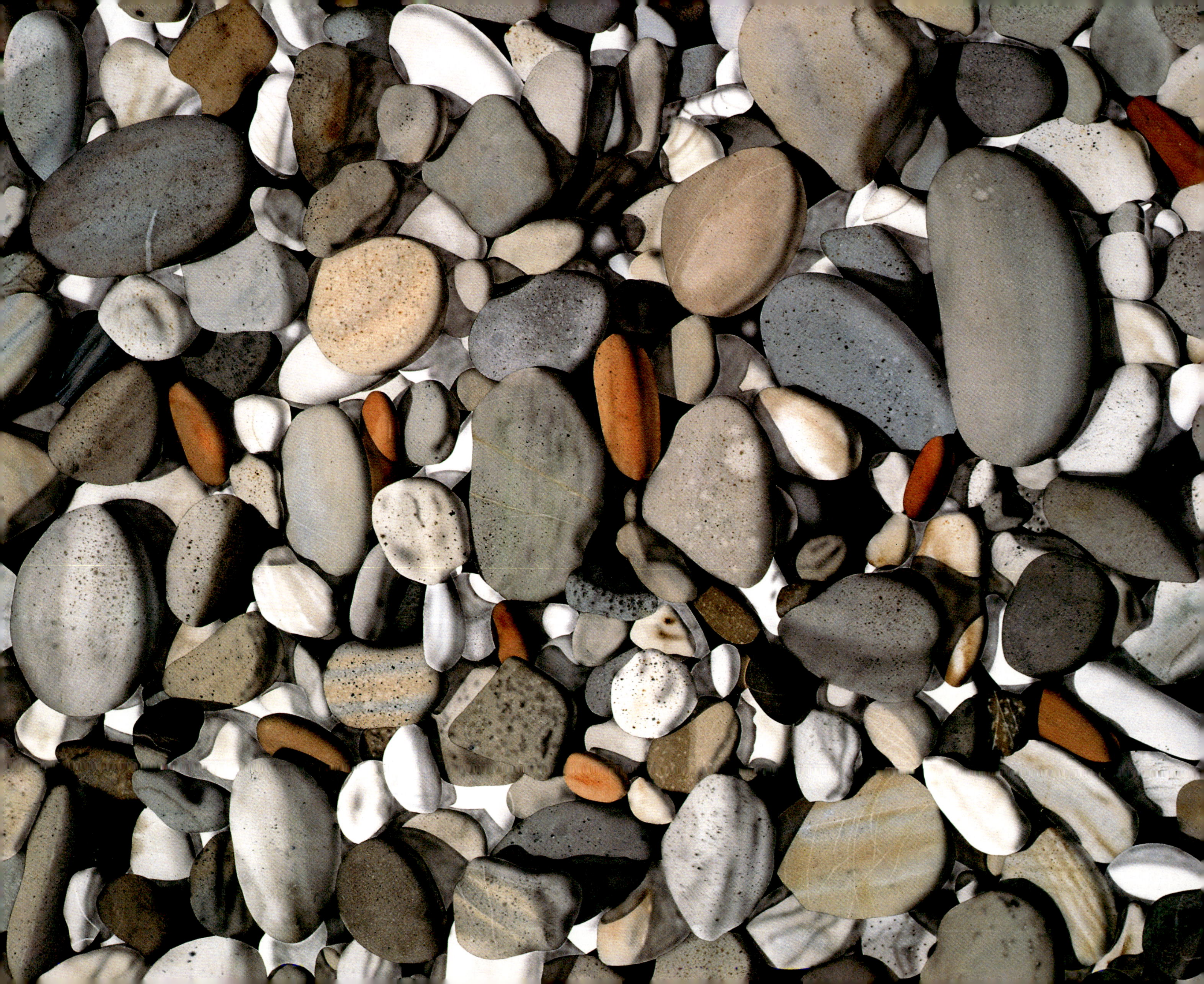

Contents

Opposite page

Title: *Elba Beach*

Year: 1990

Medium: Watercolor

Size: 40" X 60"

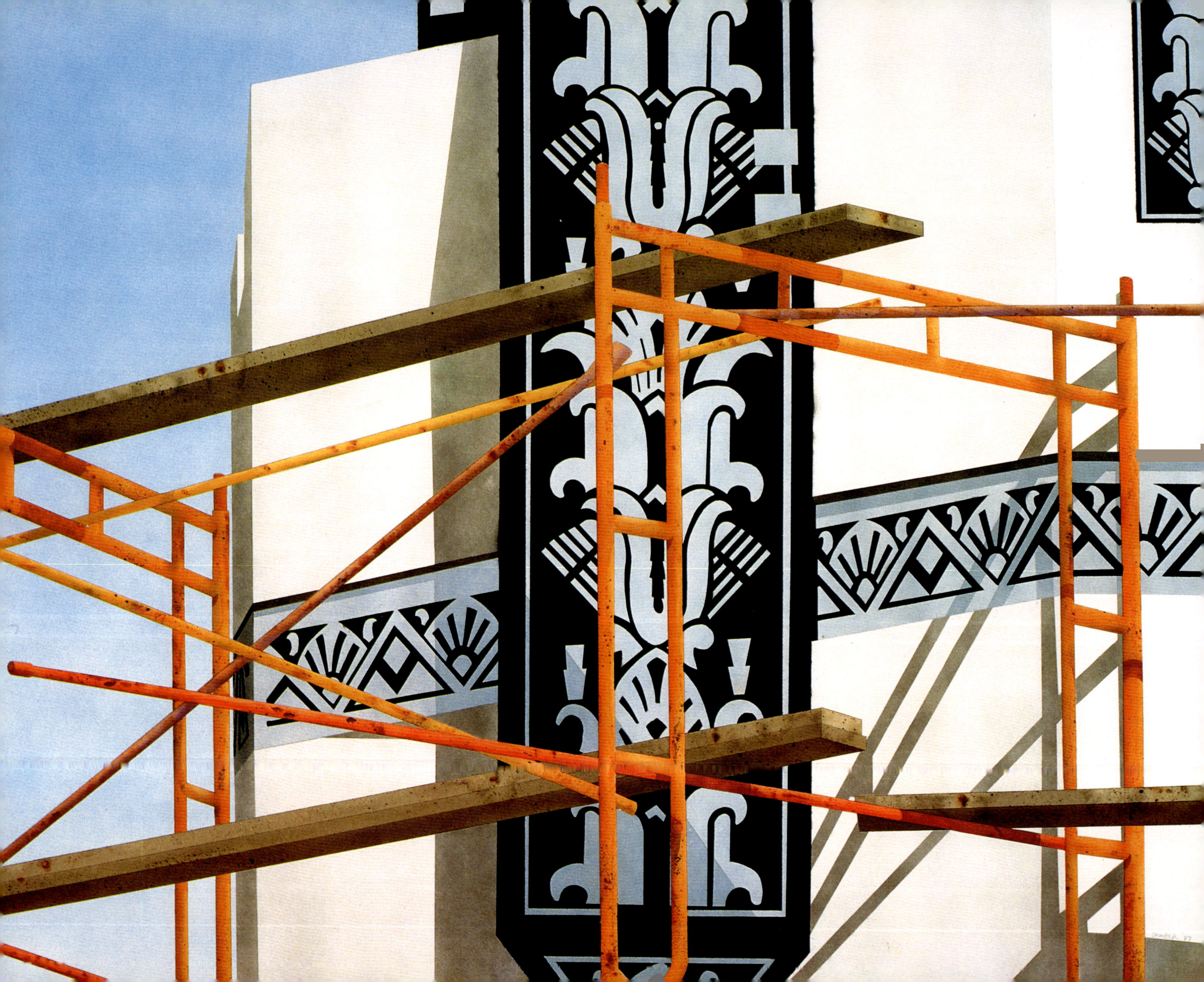

Foreword

by Townsend Wolfe and Ruth Pasquine

Generally the work of an artist changes as his interest, life or geography changes. George Dombek's subjects have varied and his technique has matured, but his point of view has remained focused and sharp. His pictures are still, but full of motion; they are realistic but abstract; they are about the mundane, but are significant; they are void of people, but have a human presence and involvement. The exploration of oppositions such as these enrich and inform the work.

George Dombek's work is deceptively simple. He tricks us into believing that his world is clear and easily understood. He does not imply or reveal totally his vision or his intent. What he does is state with clarity and precision segments and sections of the real world seen. He selects fleeting glimpses of shapes, forms and things we have walked by day after day without noticing, much less seeing or remembering. By choosing the odd angle or an unusual cropping, he focuses our attention on what we thought to be ordinary and unimportant, and causes us to see that the transitory holds a complex of meaning that is visually and experientially rich. He activates and refines our sensations. He suggests new ways of looking. He rewards our extended gaze with wonder and delight.

In the Tallahassee Jail paintings[a] Dombek focuses on an old Art Deco building undergoing restoration and covered with scaffolding. The building itself is enigmatic and full of oppositions. Its use as a jail is belied by its lavish Art Deco decoration; visually, the geometric design in the horizontal bands of etched glass contrasts with the

Opposite page

Title: *On a Clear Day*

Year: 1986

Medium: Watercolor

Size: 30" X 42"

exuberant floral motifs in the larger vertical panels. In some of the paintings, varying numbers of etched glass panels are missing because the phase of the restoration that Dombek records is the removal of the glass panels. This subtle change from picture to picture implies the constant movement that accompanies the passage of time.

In one of the works in the series, the scaffolding contrasts starkly with the building; the unabashedly utilitarian scaffolding, made out of the roughest metal and raw lumber, is rickety, and plainly not as stable as the building. Additionally, the pieces of raw lumber that provide a walkway for the workers jut out dramatically into the picture plane. One piece of lumber leans casually against a wall as if there has been a lull in the action and the workers will return any moment. The contrast between the casual, temporary scaffolding and the solidity of the building brings to mind other contradictions such as "How could such a lavish building be built to house criminals?" or "How could such a building be covered with scaffolding without being diminished?"

In another of the series, featuring a very tight, up-close view, Dombek paints the wood of the scaffolding only a shade darker than the shadows it makes against the stucco wall to set up a very active and complex pattern. He then invigorates the composition with brightly painted scaffolding of blue, yellow and orange bars that energize the picture plane with a subtle and intricate play of line, direction, and angle moving right and left, up and down, and into, as well as away from, the surface. The essential abstraction of the work is achieved with delicate membranes of color and tone which lead and direct as they control the space and movement of the composition, completely assimilating the formal qualities of the linear scaffolding and massive building.

In *On a Clear Day*, also from the Tallahassee Jail series, Dombek lovingly describes the textures and feels of the stuccoed facade and the elaborate ornament. The bright orange metal scaffolding, rusting at the edge, with odd nails protruding from the bars, is palpably felt as is the rough quality of the knotted raw lumber trusses. The scaffolding's cast shadows against the hulking building are real and add weight and substance to the scaffolding, which is delicate in comparison to the mass of the building. Light is probably the most important element in Dombek's work, and here almost a third of the picture is given over to the clear blue Florida sky. That he has used *On a Clear Day* for the exhibition title shows the importance light has for his work.

The dramatic quality of all the Tallahassee Jail paintings is achieved with cropping and a point of view which is close in and high up, as if the viewer were up on the scaffolding precariously examining some aspect of the building's facade. But the irregularity of the metal scaffolding and the myriad shadows it casts on the surface of the stucco building glistening in full sunlight are dizzying and overwhelming as we search for a firm footing. We are in the picture but not exactly sure where.

While the solidity of the work evolves from the

classical beauty of architectural form and the precise rendering of light and shade, the work goes beyond formal issues, to the building's position in time and space, altered by new relationships set up by the urge for renewal and reformation signaled by the temporary scaffolding which encompasses it. Yet the specificity of all the elements — the metal and lumber scaffolding, the slightly gritty stucco, the hot sun — grounds the work in the reality of the ordinary, as it raises the significance of everyday life.

The absence of the human element in the Tallahassee Jail series, as in most of Dombek's work, allows structure to dominate. Yet the human presence is implied by the closeness of the composition to the picture plane, the meticulous observation by the artist, the original vision of the architect, and the intervention of the renovation. The motion of activity has been silenced by the artist, allowing us to be drawn into the web of the picture to explore the complexity and find the nuance of interpretation and imagination that characterizes Dombek's work.

We are proud to honor George Dombek with this most important publication and retrospective exhibition. His artistic maturity and discipline, mastery of the watercolor medium, keen eye, and dedication are all revealed here to remind us what we might have seen if we had taken the time to look a little more closely. ■

[a]Some 20 - 25 oversized works executed in watercolor and acrylic between 1985 and 1987.

Townsend Wolfe is Director and Chief Curator and Ruth Pasquine is Curator of Art at the Arkansas Art Center.

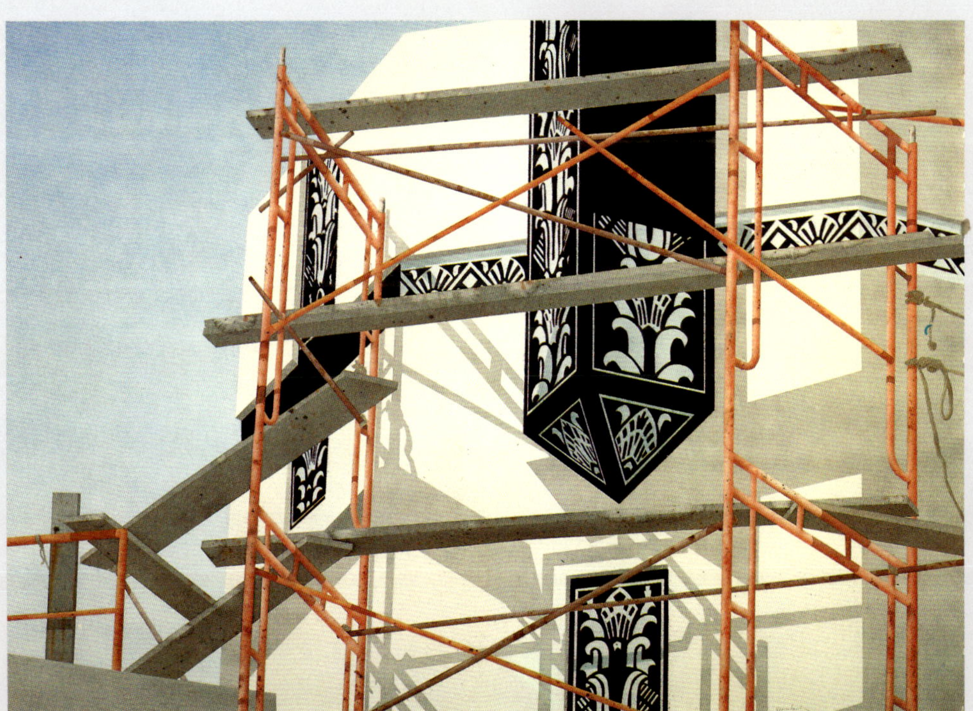

Title: *Jail #6*

Year: 1987

Medium: Watercolor

Size: 40" X 60"

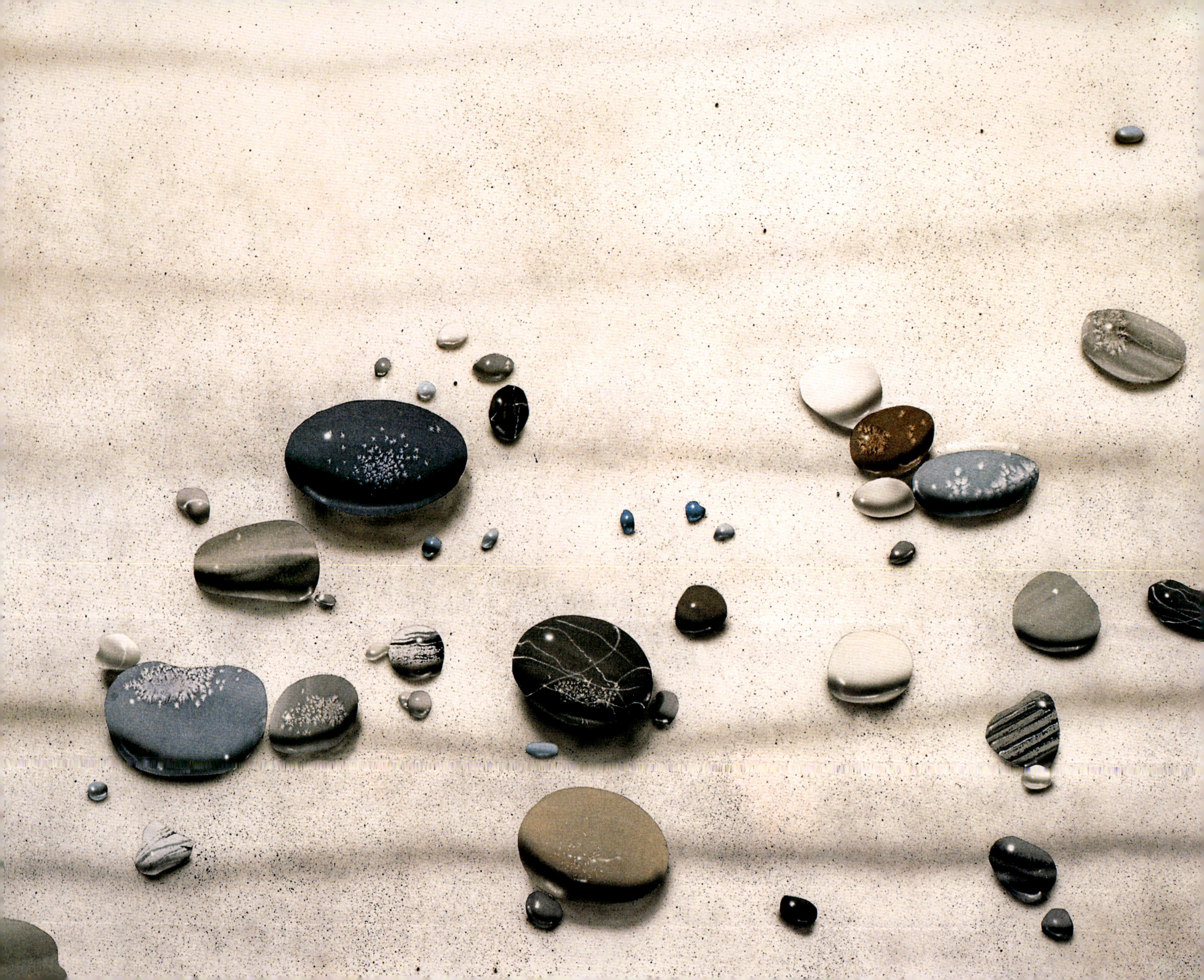

Introduction

The Paintings of George Dombek

by Donald Harington

Ironically, George Dombek has chosen for his medium a method of painting which is not ideally suited for such careful observation of real things. "If I wanted to be a photorealist," he has said, "I wouldn't use watercolors."[1]

Watercolor traditionally is loose, fluid, fast and free, and is best suited for either the kind of simplified atmospheric realism of a master like Winslow Homer, or for the emotional gestures of an expressionist like John Marin. Very few contemporary watercolorists — Philip Pearlstein with his anti-erotic nudes and William McNamara with his Ozark landscapes come to mind — are capable of using the watercolor medium with the precision and the patience that Dombek brings to it. And neither Pearlstein nor McNamara has the inclination or skill to be as meticulously exact as Dombek, whose later work is distinguishable from his earlier work primarily by the heightened degree of technical facility; an ever-diminishing brushstroke and an ever-increasing faithfulness to optical truth.

Early in his student days, Dombek spent a lot of time practicing the tricky medium of watercolor by imitating, in what he calls his beginner's "slap-dash"

Opposite page

Title: *The Cinque Terre*

Year: 1991

Medium: Watercolor

Size: 30" X 42"

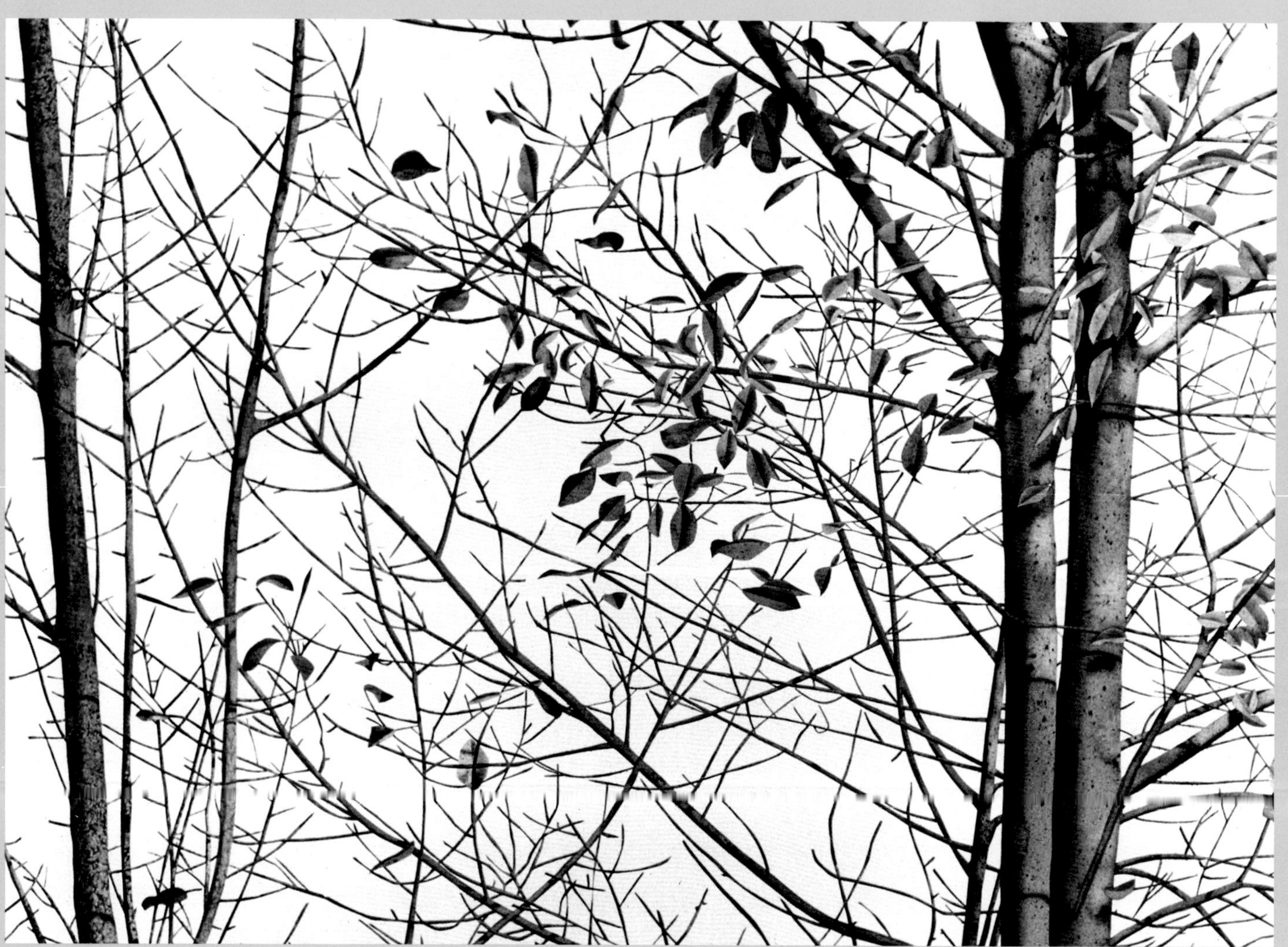

Title: *Two Trees*

Year: 1991

Medium: Watercolor

Size: 30" X 42"

style, the work of virtuosos like Homer and Marin, as well as Maurice Prendergast, Charles Burchfield, John Singer Sargent, and Andrew Wyeth — all American masters of the watercolor medium but all of them, with the possible exception of Wyeth, working in a spontaneous manner that was essentially alien to Dombek's vision and temperament. Not until he took a degree in architecture and carried over the architect's tools to his painting did Dombek remove the impulsive gesture from his painting and replace it with a highly controlled sense of organization.

Searching for clues to the essential Dombek temperament which rejects spontaneity and impulsiveness, we discover that Dombek's mother was a quilt maker. On a small farm outside the town of Paris in western Arkansas where he was born in 1944, his mother raised a large family — George has four brothers and a sister — and devoted her free time to restless handicrafts, embroidering doilies and other needlework as well as piecing together and stitching traditional quilts. Dombek's most vivid memories are of watching her at this meticulous, patient labor. His most valued possessions today are half a dozen of his mother's best quilts. He says, "Often times when I pick up a pair of scissors I can't help but think of her."[2]

But his mother's quilts, even if their regularity and geometry predict the direction of George Dombek's art, were not of her own invention; she was like a musician who devotes a methodical talent to the playing of someone else's composition. Dombek may have acquired from her his nimble fingers and the infinite perseverance to stick with a task for days and weeks and months. He may credit her for his genuine liking of constant sustained labor, but not necessarily for the creative imagination that transforms the raw material into art.

His father, a coal miner, slowly developed black

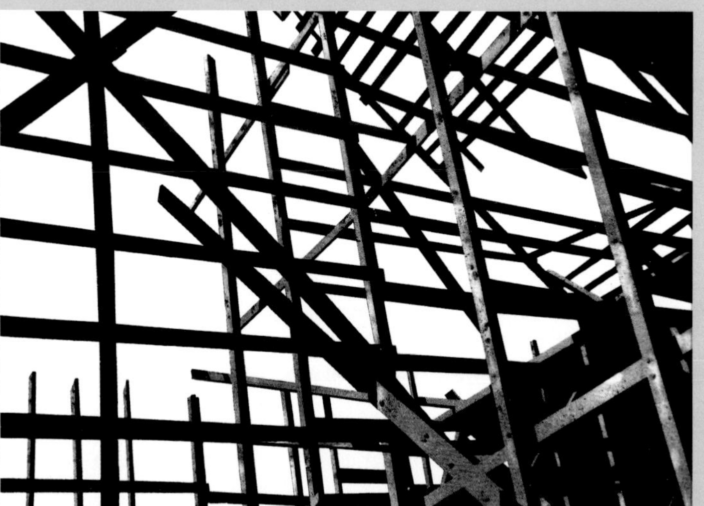

Title: *To the Sun*

Year: 1986

Medium: Watercolor

Size: 22" X 30"

lung, the disease that would eventually kill him. The coal mines of Arkansas flourished in the '40s and '50s and gave rise to towns with names like Coal Hill. Today they are abandoned.

The small Dombek farm was a half-mile from the mine where George's father worked, ironically called "The Jewel." The mine's large dump was a favorite playground of young George and possibly a source of the deep blacks that dominate his palette. The farm also bordered the Arkansas wilderness, where George often escaped, alone, to indulge his curiosity for the geometries of nature — spider webs, fish scales, wasp nests, rock formations and the endless calligraphics of trees and flowers. Yet that wilderness, like most of Arkansas itself, was not a rationally ordered world, certainly not a "civilized" place. Quite possibly young George sought out those little geometries as some kind of assurance, if not security. He thus acquired at a very early age, long before his discovery of such a thing as "art," the sense of the conflict between order and chaos, between planning and happening, between logical mind and irrational feeling.

He was a long time in discovering art, and learning that art confirms, even glorifies, these conflicts. Before the age of 17, by his recollection, he had never seen an original work of art, never set foot in a museum, and certainly never knew any artists, not even architects. At 18 he saw some art reviews in *Time* magazine, some stuff about some guys named Pollock and Kline, and, like so any neophyte artists as well as the scornful public, he sought to prove that "anybody can do that." His imitation Pollocks and Klines failed to convince him that anybody could do that; he certainly couldn't do that. Even in Pollock's most turbulent accidents or Kline's boldest splashes of the housepainter's brush, George Dombek perceived that there was some kind of artistic control at work, a kind of control that would require an education.

As a high school junior George signed up for the only art course offered, whose teacher taught a variety of media, starting with watercolor, a technique that George fell in love with on the spot and never gave up.

From high school he went to Arkansas State Teachers College in Conway, where he attempted to major in commercial art but failed all of his courses, changed his major to math, the only subject he had liked in high school, but failed again, and left school. Drifting for five years through a succession of jobs,

George worked mostly in construction labor, building pipelines, highways and houses, helping to arrange man's geometry on the surface of the earth.

Finally, at the age of 25, without having met a single architect, he decided to enroll in the School of Architecture at the University of Arkansas in Fayetteville. His teachers there, including the distinguished architect Fay Jones, "were saying things that he desperately needed to hear,"[3] and kept him constantly busy with projects. However, in the summers he would sneak over to the Art Department to take courses in watercolor from Robert Ross and Neppie Conner.

After he achieved his bachelor's degree in architecture he was accepted into the Master of Fine Arts program in art, where he spent three years, primarily with Ross as his mentor. ■

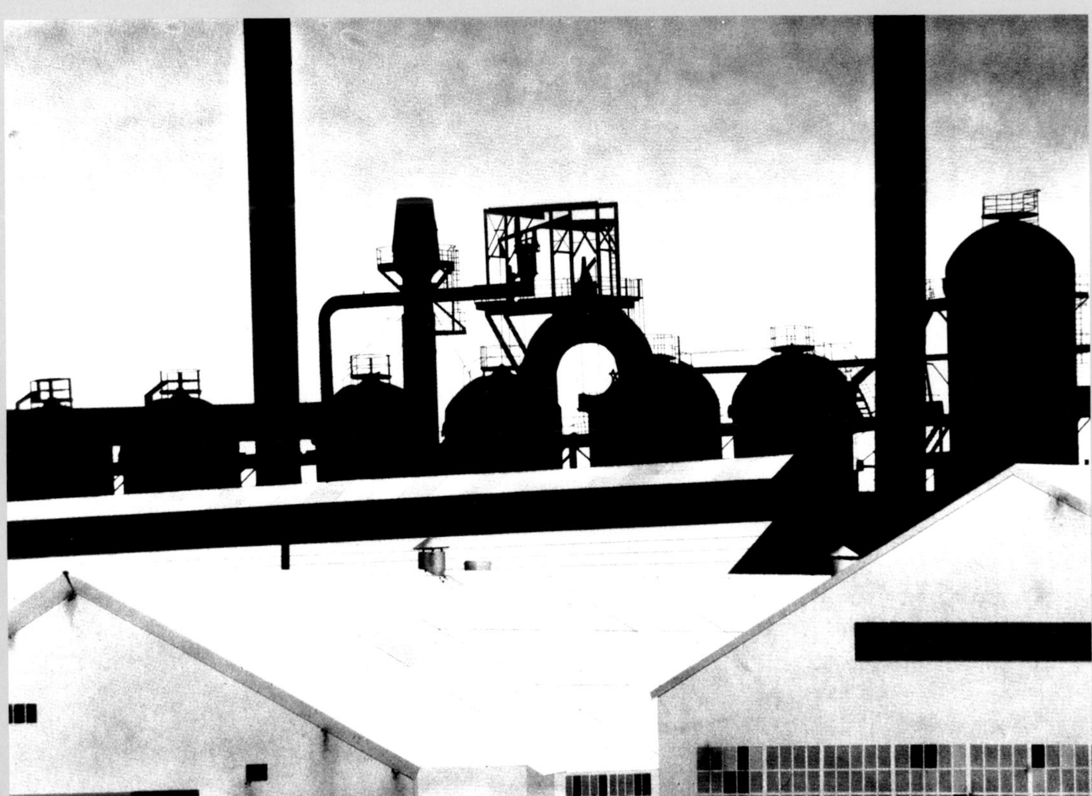

Title: *Steel Mill South*

Year: 1986

Medium: Watercolor

Size: 30" X 42"

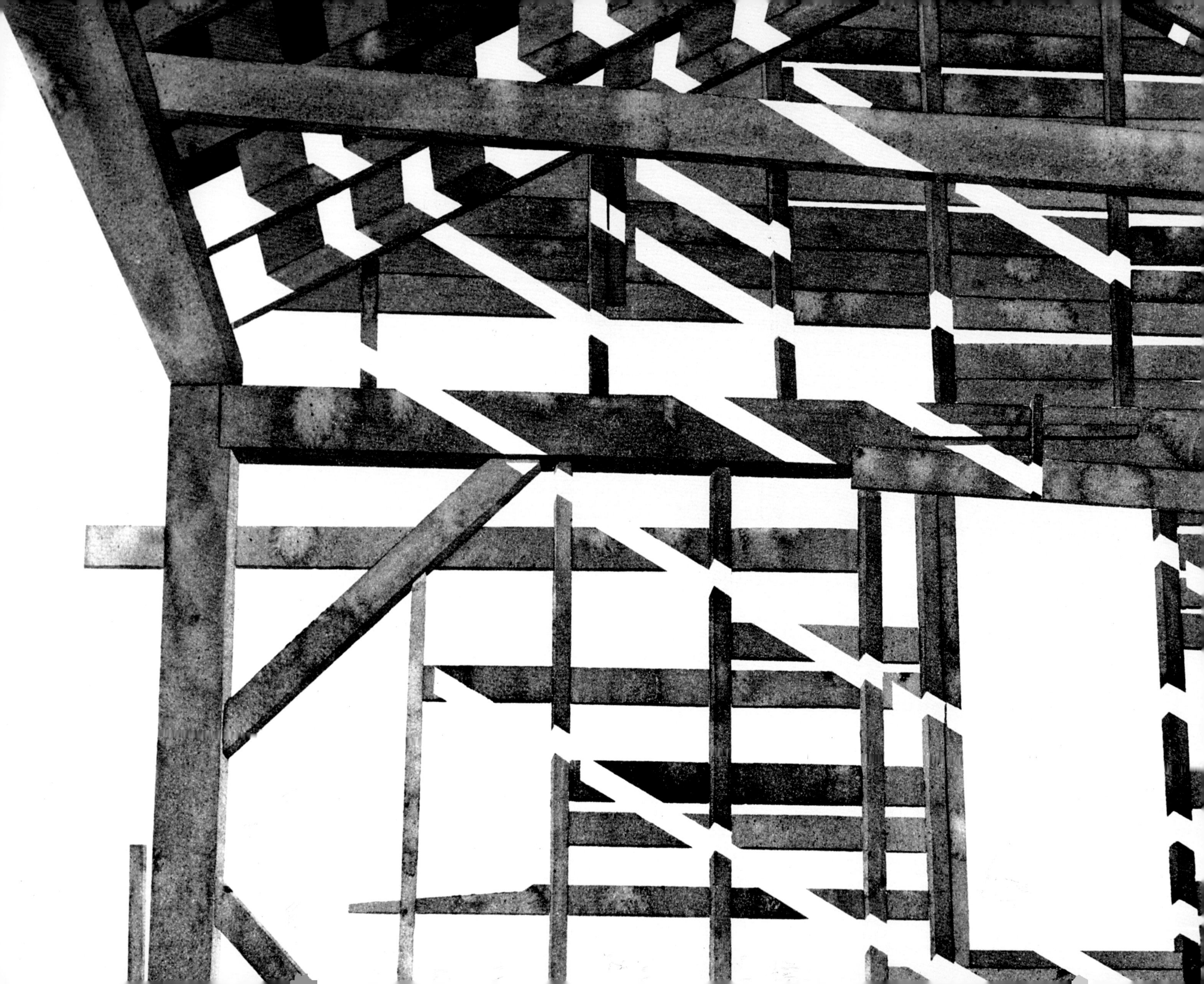

Series One

Arkansas Barns

1975 - 1977

Midway through Dombek's graduate studies in art, after doing hundreds of watercolors in his "slap-dash" style, he grew nostalgic for the precise instruments of the architect, and began to use them: straight-edge and T-square and triangle. A course in architectural preservation had exposed him to the decaying barns of the Ozarks, which brought back memories of the hours he'd worked and played in the Arkansas family barn. He began to envision for his master's thesis the suite of watercolors that he called "White Series," but which he now calls simply "Crates," for that is what they are: common wooden-slatted vegetable crates tossed or piled in a barn.

One of these watercolors hangs prominently in the main library of the University of Arkansas, a part of its permanent collection, a distinction that very few of the "thesis paintings" by the Art Department's M.F.A. students have earned.

In his thesis statement,[4] Dombek is careful to point out that the "subject matter" of these crates has no meaning for him; he is clearly concerned only with their visual design, their geometry, the patterns of shadows, the negative and positive spaces of light and

Opposite page

Title: *Washington County Barn*

Year: 1976

Medium: Watercolor

Size: 28" X 38"

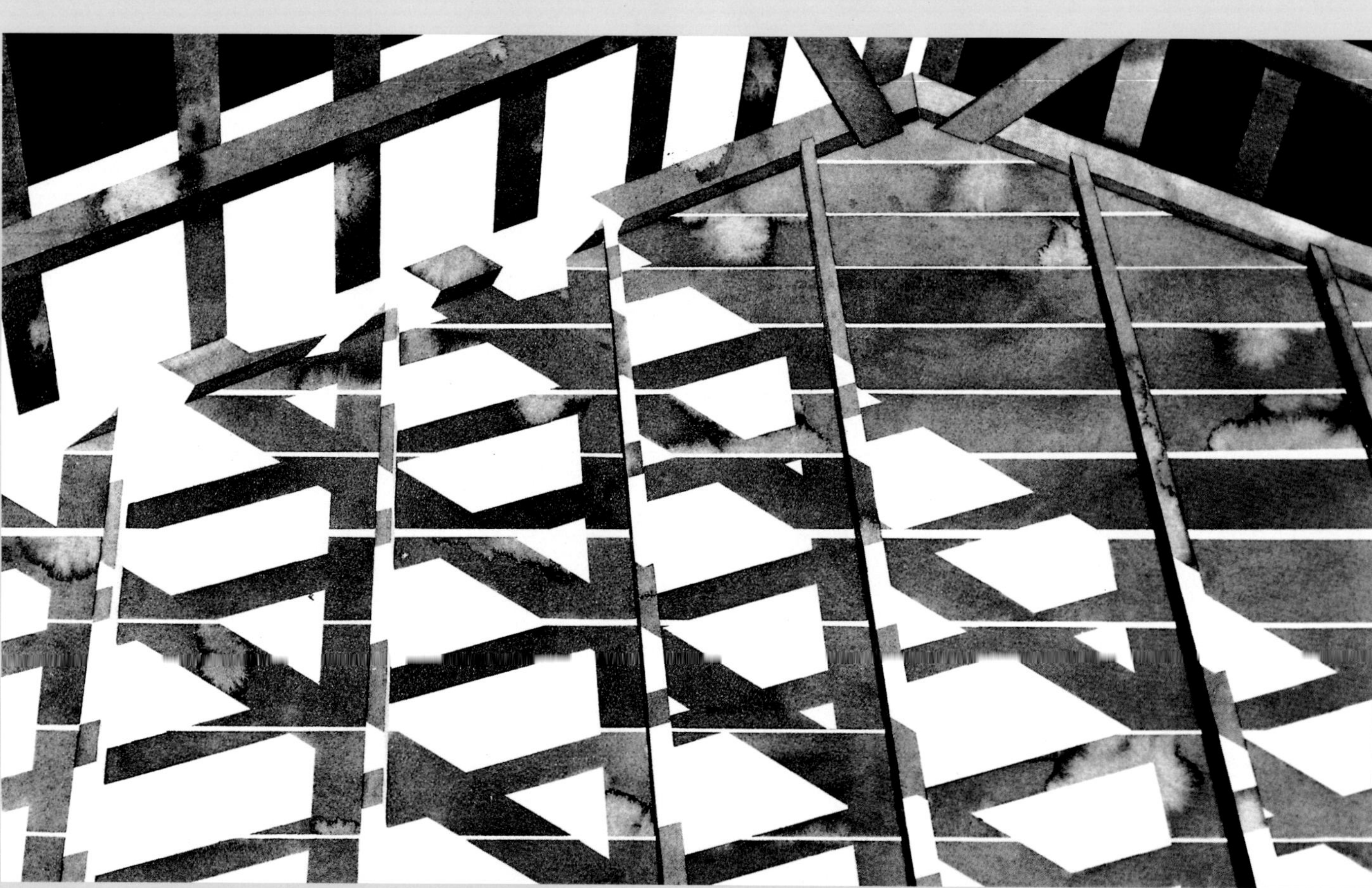

Title: *Grid Work*

Year: 1977

Medium: Watercolor

Size: 28" X 38"

dark, the purely formal qualities of the "visual experience," as Dombek refers repeatedly to the act of seeing.

There is no connection between the "subject matter" of the banana and the crates, for they are not banana crates. The bananas do not "belong" to the scene; they are clearly contrivances planted in the scene by the artist, to assert the artist's presence and the viewer's awareness that the artist is in charge, not merely a recorder of optical reality but a manipulator of it. This concept is reinforced by the presence of the light fixture, a common clamp-on lamp of the type used to illuminate a still-life in the studio. Its serpentine electrical cord, dangling down the picture plane, is a foil to the rigid geometry of the crates, just as the curves of the bananas, as well as their yellow color, are counterpoints to the painting's gray complexity of diagonal straight lines.

In this painting Dombek manifests, for the first time, the theme that he will return to again in some of his later work: the romance of roundness as a relief from the rigidity of the rectangle. But he was

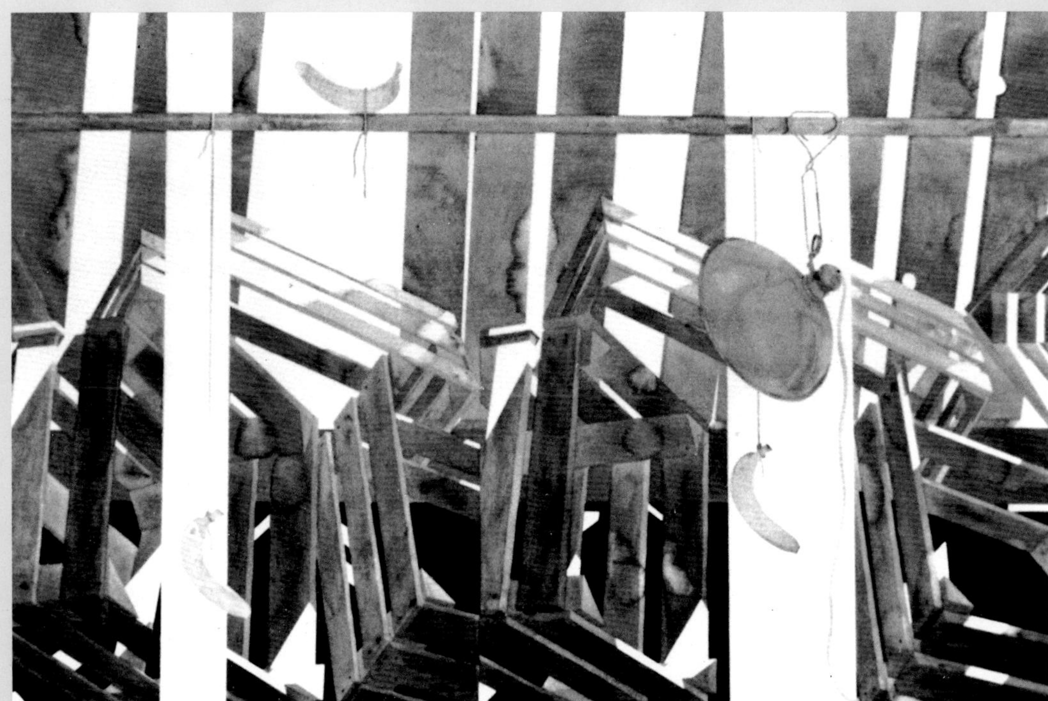

Title: *Crates*

Year: 1977

Medium: Watercolor

Size: 42" X 72"

Title: *Barn Crates*

Year: 1975

Medium: Watercolor

Size: 16" X 21"

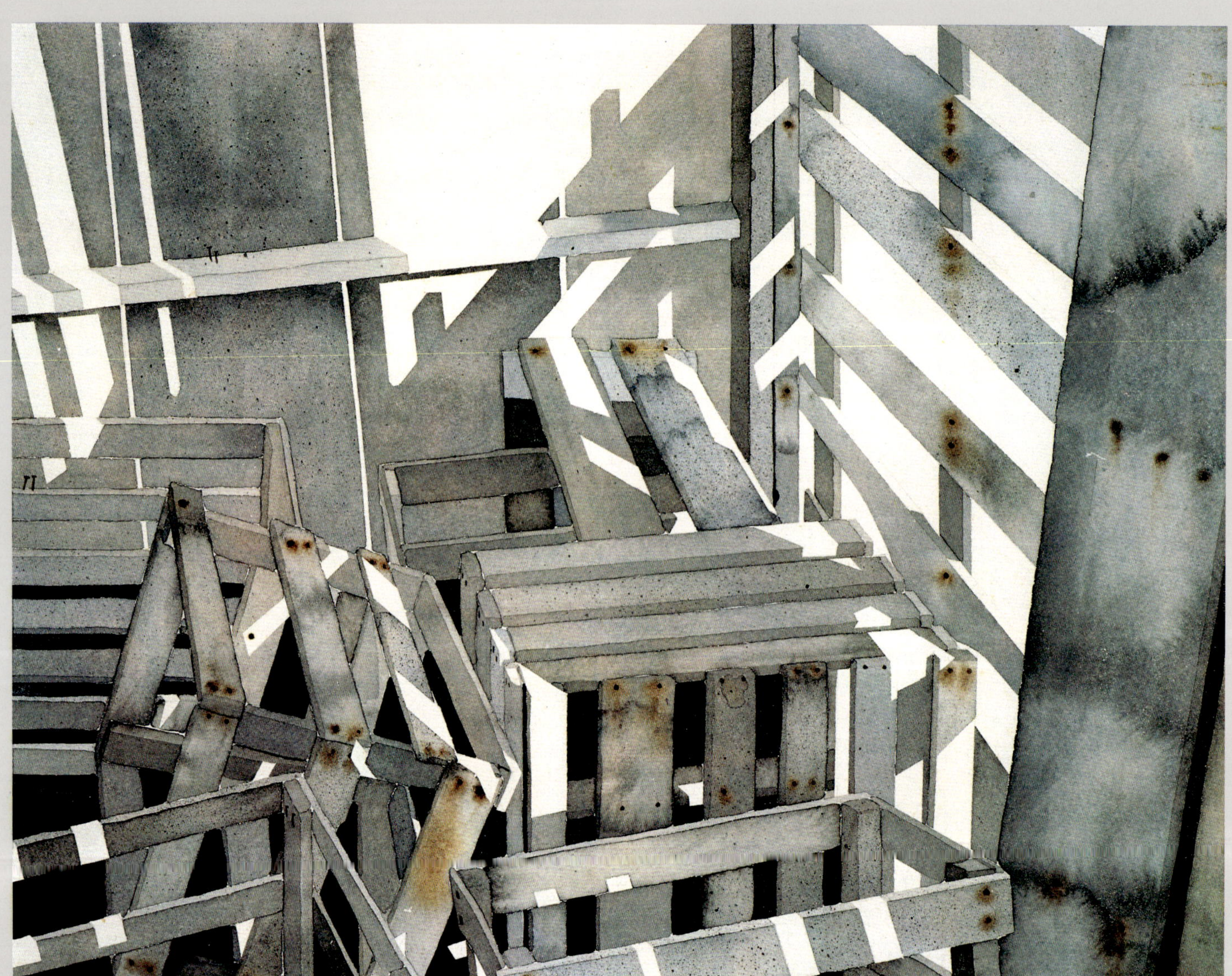

not happy with the painting. "The fourth painting did not bring into existence a rich complexity of images as I had hoped," he wrote in his thesis, "but one of confusion."[5]

Dombek spent one semester working under Donald Roller Wilson, then a member of the art department faculty and not yet famous for his meticulously realistic fantasies. He feels he may have incorporated the banana and lamp into the picture under the influence of Wilson, or at least the indirect impact of Wilson's ideas about "storytelling as opposed to visual phenomena."[6] In all of his mature work, even the recent, charming *Blue Stick Bike in Tree*, Dombek has rejected the idea that his pictures should tell stories.

However, Dombek would conclude after years of avoiding it, "I can say I am not as sure about the 'insignificance of subject matter' as I once was." [7] ■

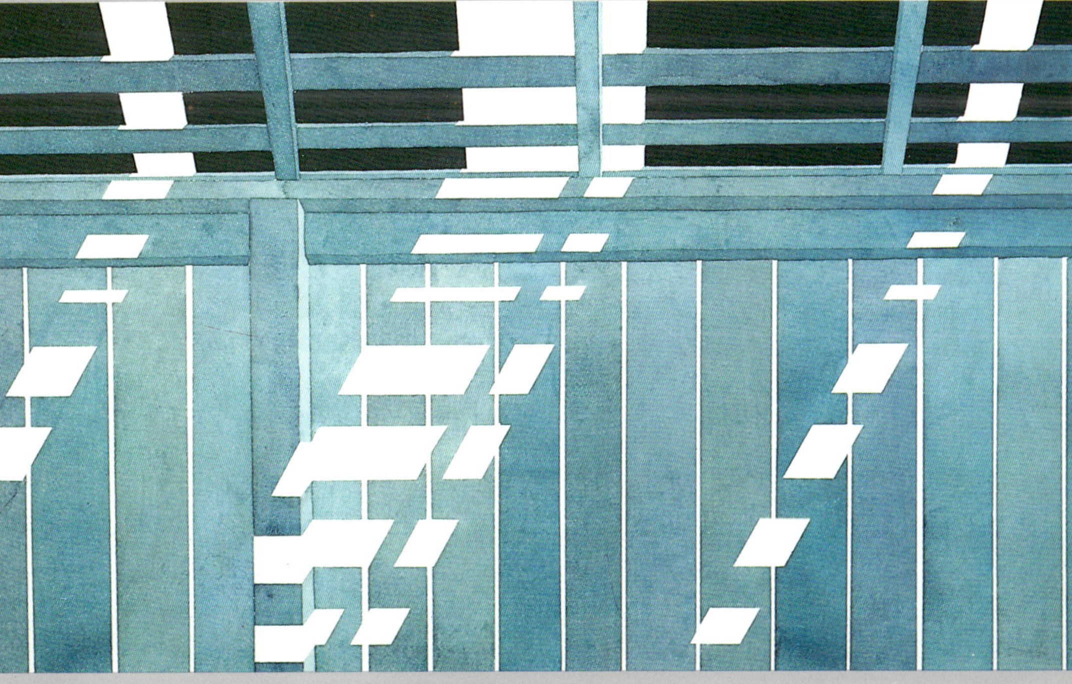

Title: *Barn Lines*

Year: 1976

Medium: Watercolor

Size: 24" X 38"

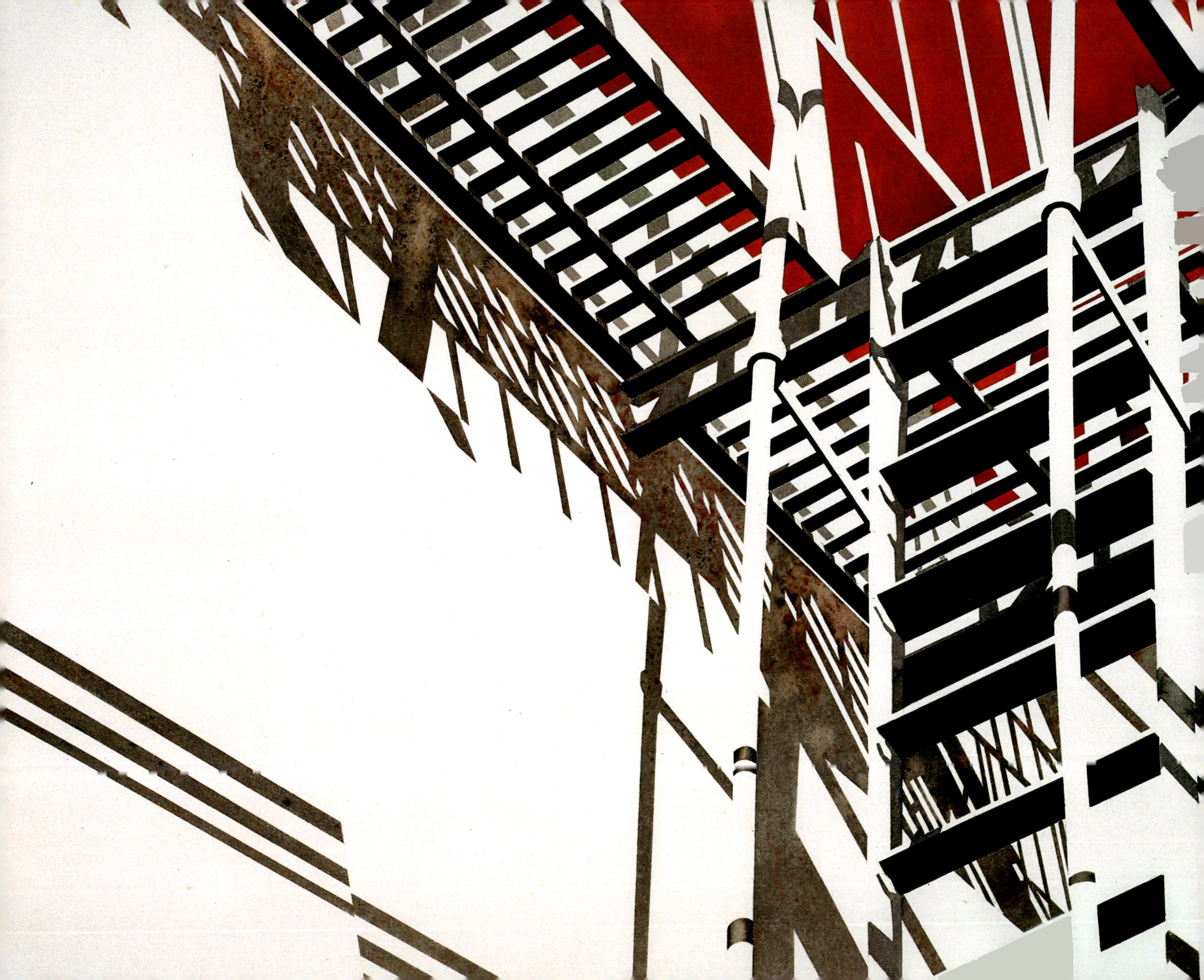

Series Two

San Francisco Fire Escapes

1977 - 1979

After receiving his master's in painting from the University of Arkansas, Dombek moved to San Francisco and began work as an architect, but continued painting in his free time, sometimes all night. He made two important discoveries: the monumental work of contemporary artists and the availability of watercolor paper in continuous rolls. Together, these two findings inspired him to attempt ten-foot long paintings.

He missed the weathered barns of the Ozarks, those airy structures where sunlight piercing the gaps between boards had fascinated him with the revelation that the shadow of a thing is often more important than the thing itself. In San Francisco he discovered the big city's substitute for this visual experience: the fire escape.

Dombek was to spend more than two years painting fire escapes, beginning his habit of apparent single-mindedness: picking a subject and doing it again and again. But despite the attempt of critics to find significance in this subject matter, here was a classic instance of Dombek's indifference to "meaning," his insistence upon pure aesthetic visual qualities: his excitement at the introduction of several

Opposite page

Title: *San Francisco Fire Escape*

Year: 1977

Medium: Watercolor

Size: 30" X 42"

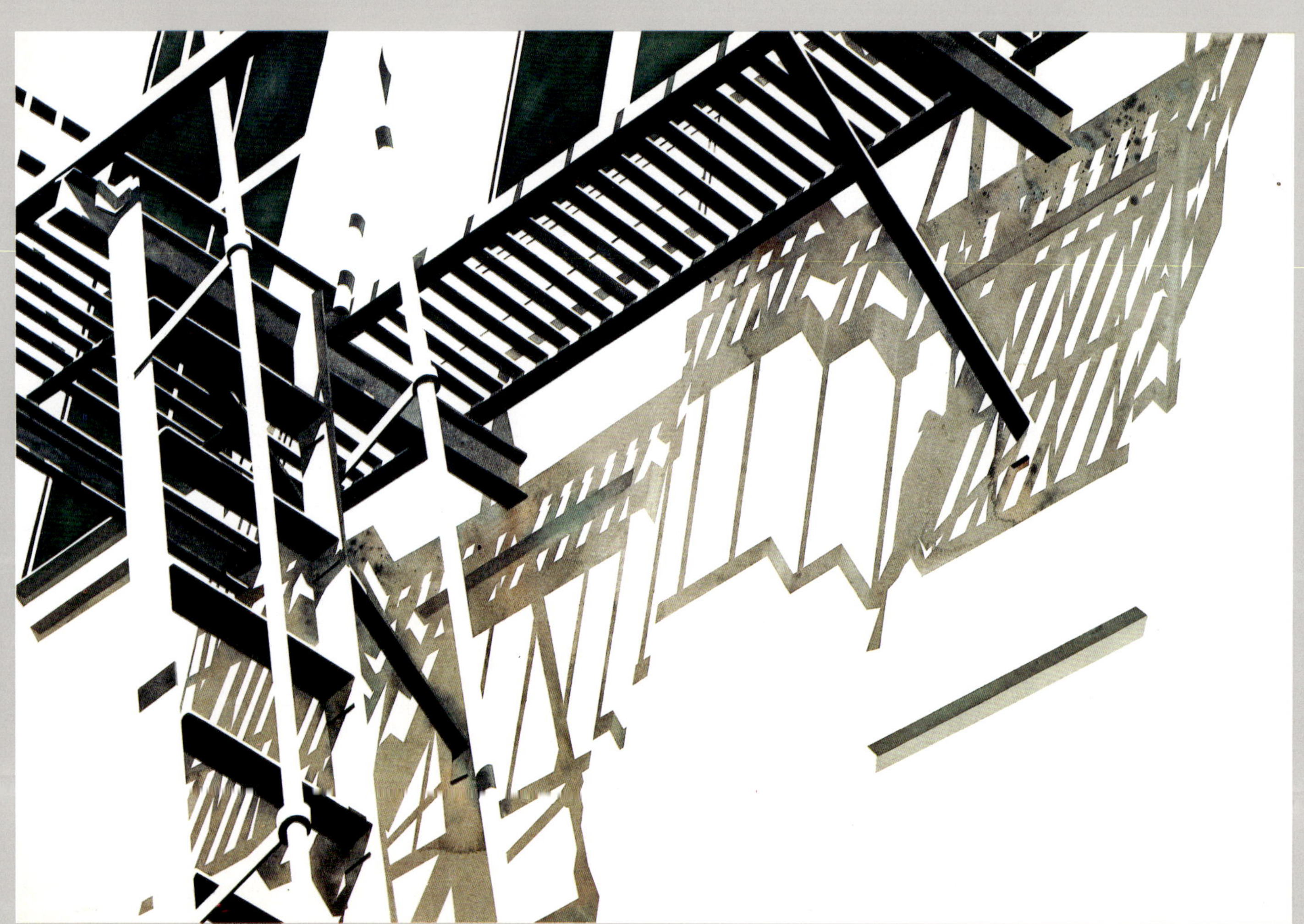

Title: *San Francisco Windows*

Year: 1978

Medium: Watercolor

Size: 38" X 58"

new elements to the repertoire of form that had begun in the Ozark barns and vegetable crates: the rhythms of successive parallel diagonals, the opposition of diagonals and the tilting-back of the perspective, an ever-stronger sunlight which tends to destroy structure and leave only its shadow, and, most strikingly, a new sense of color.

This color has fooled some critics into associations with fire itself. In an essay accompanying the first major Dombek retrospective, at the Butler Institute of American Art in 1988, art historian Betty Rogers Rubenstein wrote, "Now, new and brilliant colors appear, harsh red and orange tones that suit the iconography of fire escapes — colors that register emergency, danger and fear."[8] Dr. Rubenstein was accurate in her observation that these colors project a sharp contrast to the soft weathered grays of those White Series vegetable crates, but the "fire" colors of Dombek's fire escapes really have nothing to do with emergency, danger or fear; indeed, the feeling of these paintings almost contradicts any associations with fire or with escape: there is a sense of order, of clarity and precision, of permanence and timelessness, which give Dombek's art a new power, perhaps a sense of design and form that he would never again realize with quite as much discipline.

These fire escapes would afford Dombek his first popular recognition. The William Sawyer Gallery gave Dombek his first one-man show, which attracted considerable attention from journalistic critics in the *San Francisco Examiner,* the *San Francisco Chronicle,* and *Art Voices South*. Reviewer Ann Heymann concluded, "Since viewing Dombek's fire escapes, one finds oneself looking with much interest and curiosity at real ones, and have found they don't even run a close second."[9]

Those words offer a clue to the secret of

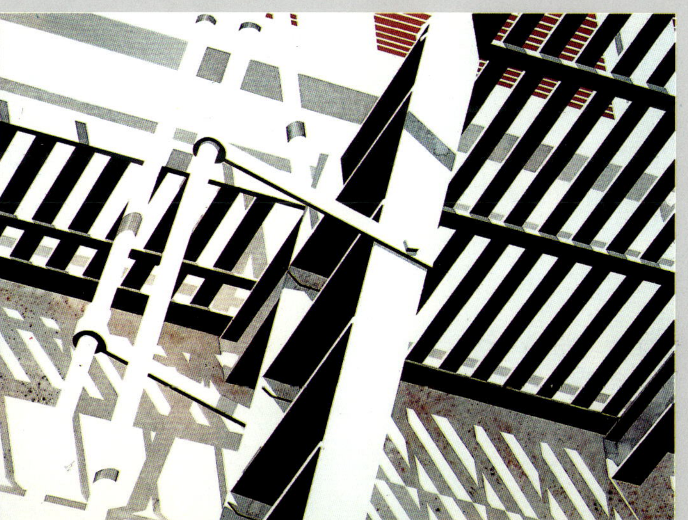

Title: *Clay Street*

Year: 1978

Medium: Watercolor

Size: 28" X 40"

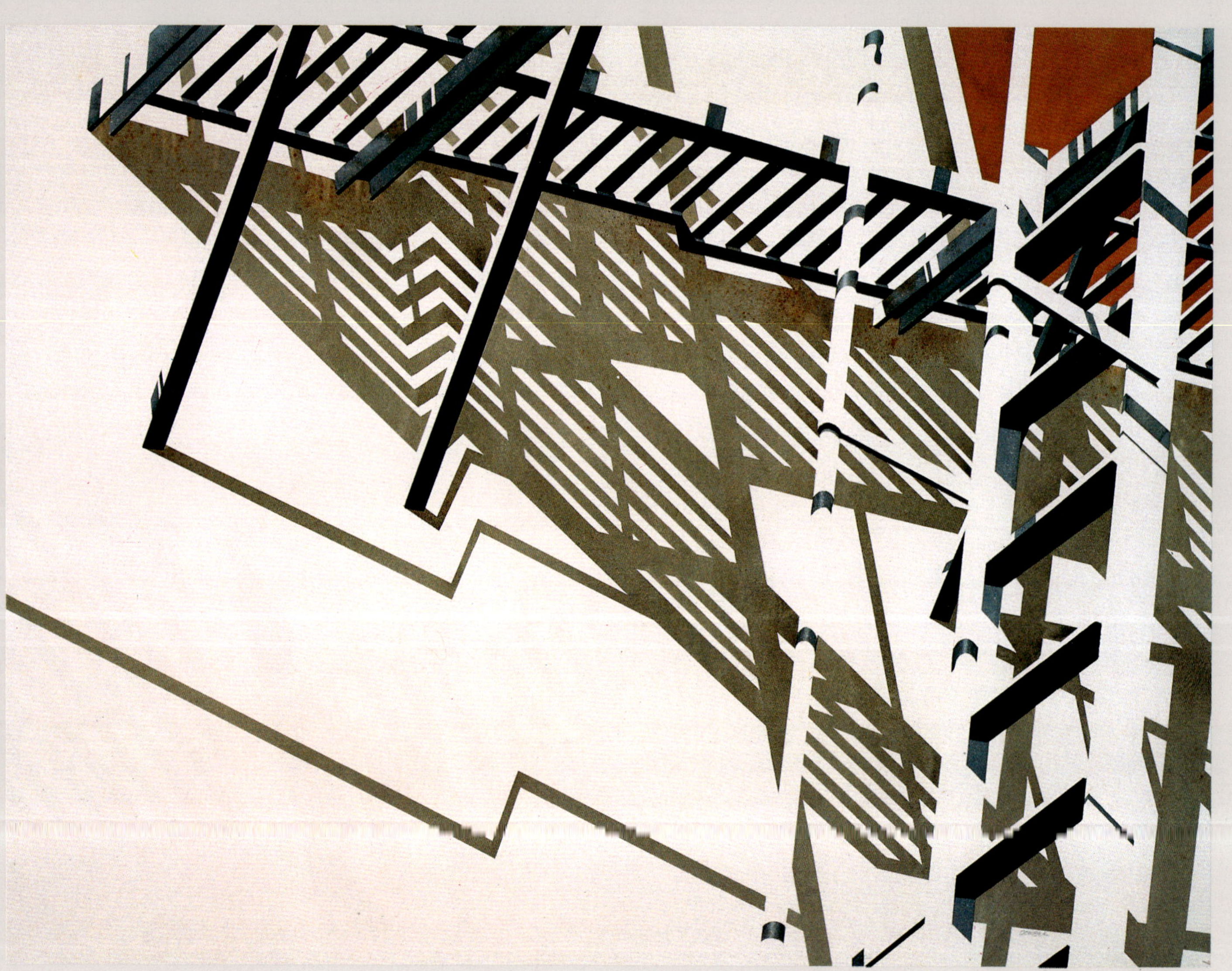

Title: *Pine & Baker*

Year: 1977

Medium: Watercolor

Size: [illegible]" X [illegible]"

Dombek's success: starting with the humble vegetable crates and continuing, years later, with the lowly bicycles made of sticks, Dombek has the talent to take unpretentious objects from the visible world and make us notice them, make us aware of their interest and integrity as forms.

Although the show was not a financial success, and Dombek learned a painful truth as well, "There is not a large buying public that will invest in watercolors," [10] the reviewers' praise was enough to persuade Dombek to devote himself to his painting. He quit his architectural job and accepted a position as visiting artist at Youngstown State University. ■

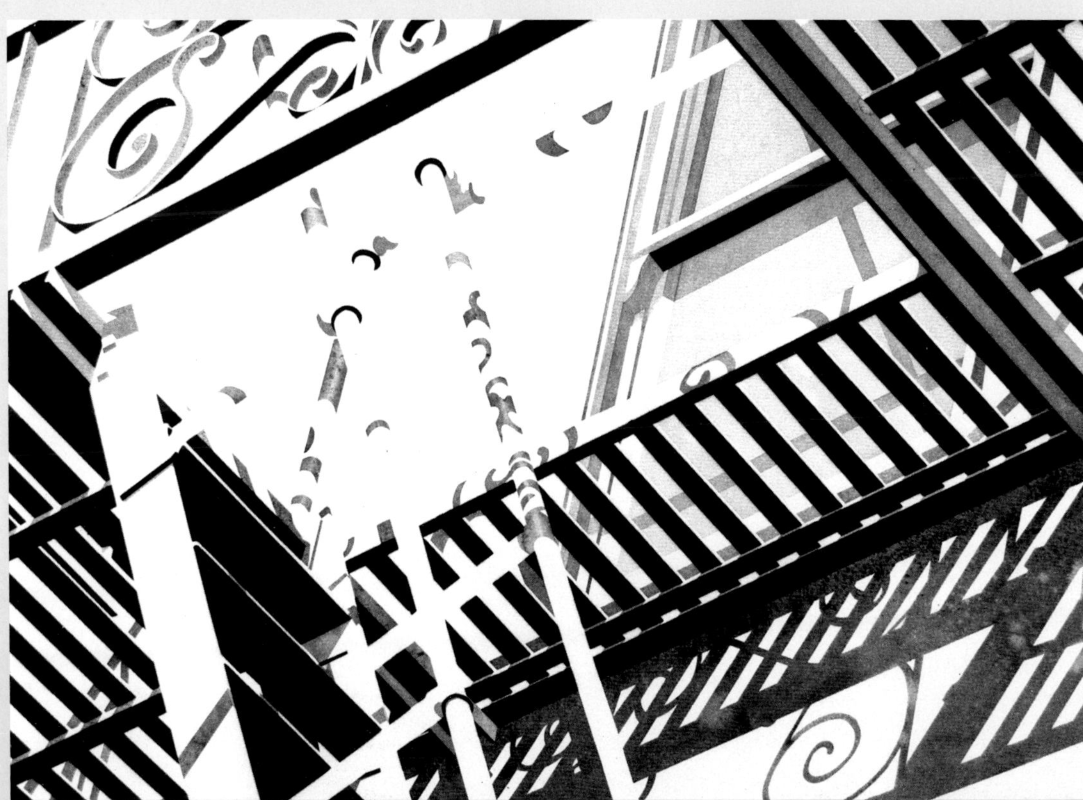

Title: *Baker & Clay*

Year: 1978

Medium: Watercolor

Size: 40" X 60"

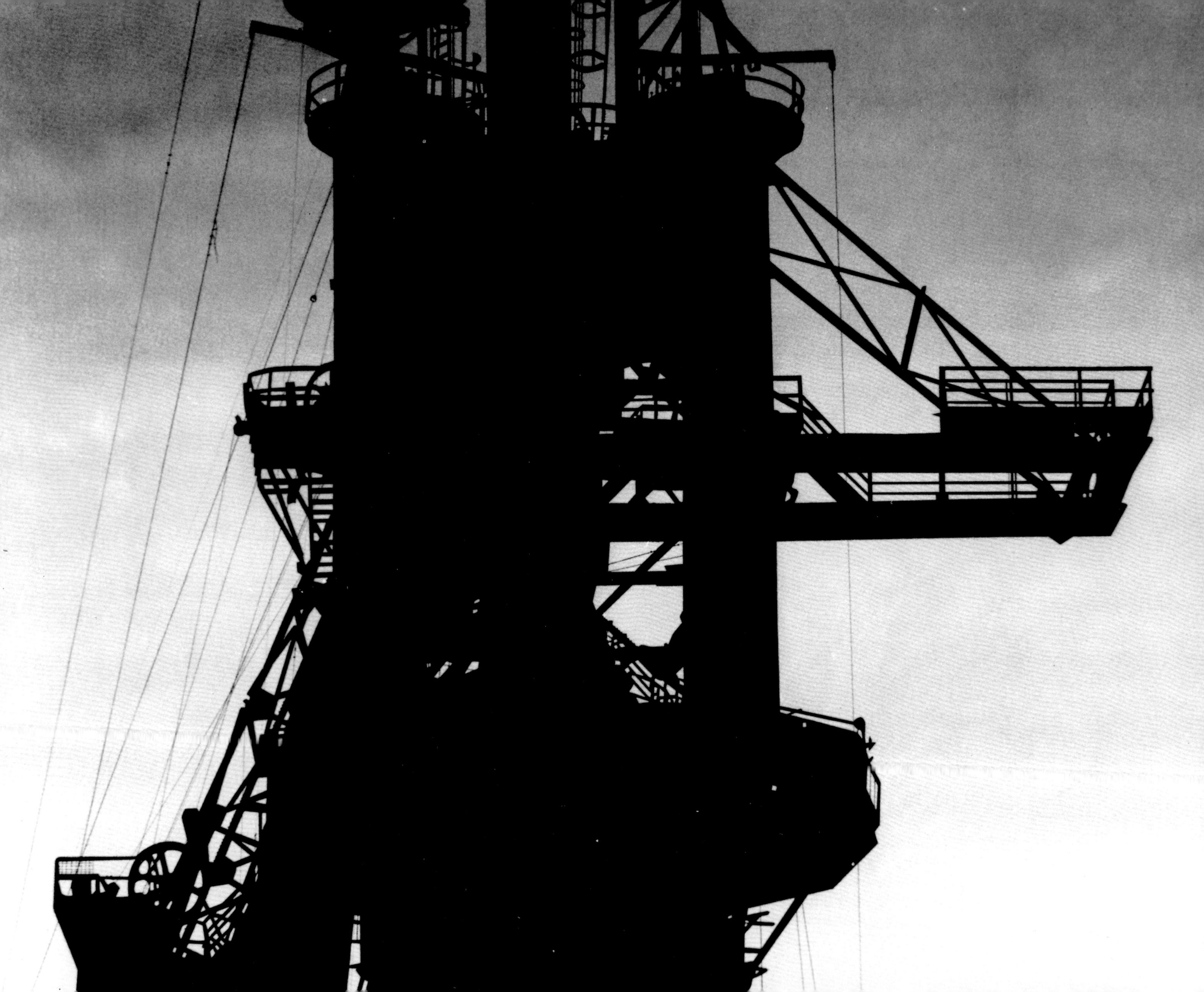

Series Three

Youngstown Steel Mills

1979 - 1986

Youngstown was a city of giant steel mills which were in the process of being shut down when George Dombek arrived, reminding him of the Arkansas coal mines. The black which had dominated his palette from the first moment he realized the strength of shadow now exploded into his consciousness. He learned his father was dying from black lung, he knew the black coal mines were closed for good, he watched the black steel foundries become cold and useless, and he had an "awareness of a disappearing landscape"[11] which prompted a new kind of painting: still geometric and still "real," but abandoning light and pattern and color.

Since Dombek worked from his own photographs instead of on site, and since his photographs of the steel mills have the same artistic qualities as those of Charles Sheeler and Edward Weston, he was able to return to the subject of the Youngstown mill again and again, almost every year

Title: *Youngstown Steel Mill*

Year: 1979

Medium: Watercolor

Size: 16" X 20"

after his short stay at Youngstown State, and to "preserve" that "iron landscape."[12] The natural landscape reminded him of northwest Arkansas and drew him back to Ohio repeatedly, and on one of these return visits he met the woman who was to become his wife, Karen, a native of the Youngstown area.

So the Youngstown pictures, of all his work, have the greatest potential for being meaningful in terms of subject matter, and that is certainly true of those stark, all-black configurations which transform the mills into silhouettes of monsters. These mills closed for the same reason the Arkansas coal mines shut down: they were technologically outmoded. Dombek's rendering of them underscores their antiquated obsolescence, like some extinct dinosaurs leaving behind not their fossils but only their shadows.

The steel mill forms are basically flattened shapes parallel to the picture plane, yet contrast the previous two series, the crates and the fire escapes. The forms are at a distance from the observer, and thus the cropping is not as essential, and the resulting compositions lack the music of the earlier work; the rhythmic slat is replaced by the looming monolithic machine. But the powerful interplay between positive and negative space, which distinguishes all of Dombek's work, is given a bold new direction by the Kline-like play of dark against light.

Thus, the steel mill pictures may be the most subjectively meaningful of his themes, but they are at the same time the most purely "abstract." They paved the way for the most impressive of Dombek's images, the tobacco barn series. ■

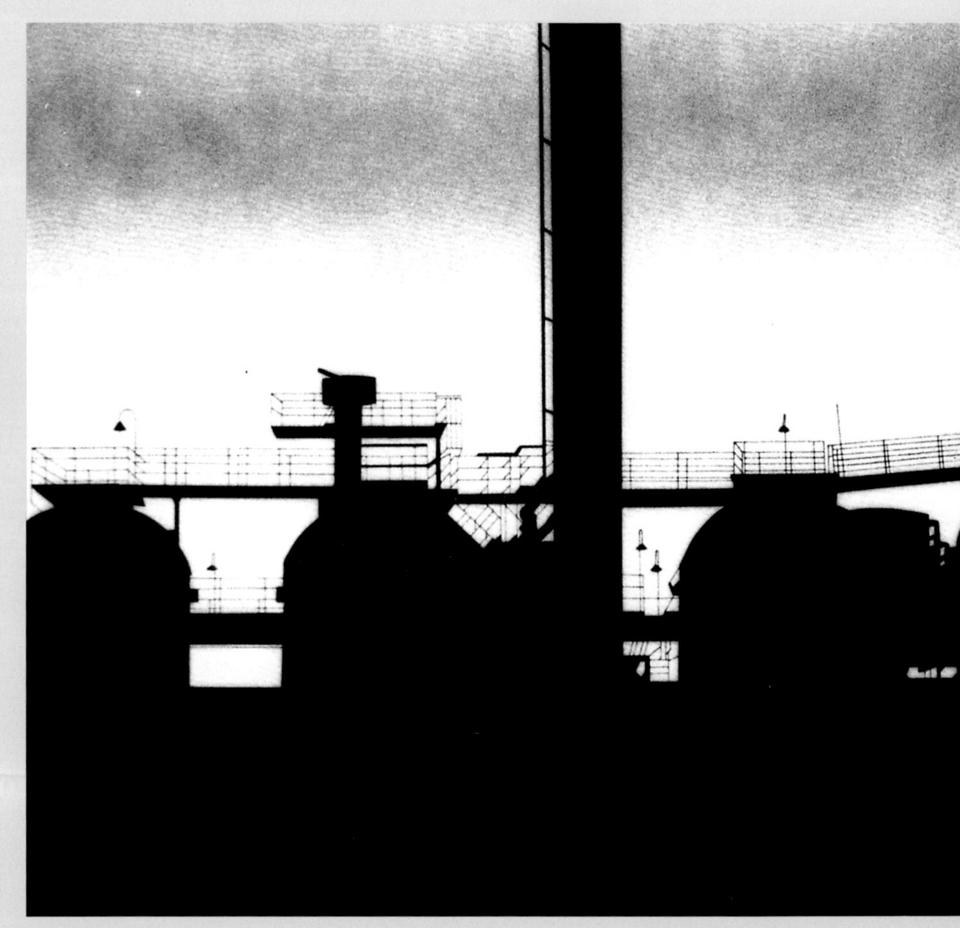

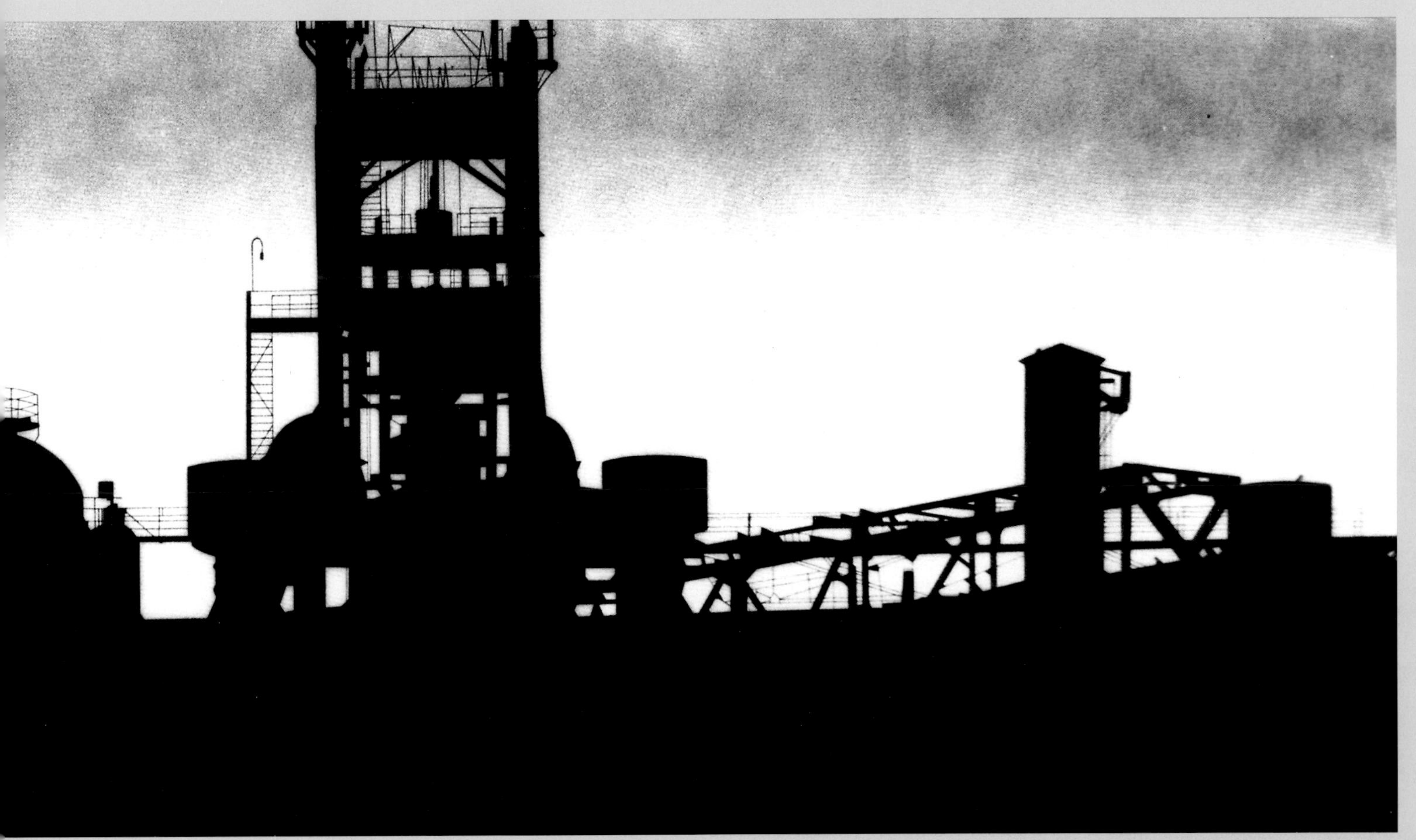

Title: *New Center Street Bridge*

Year: 1986

Medium: Watercolor

Size: 24" X 60"

Title: *Republic Steel*

Year: 1986

Medium: Watercolor

Size: 30" X 42"

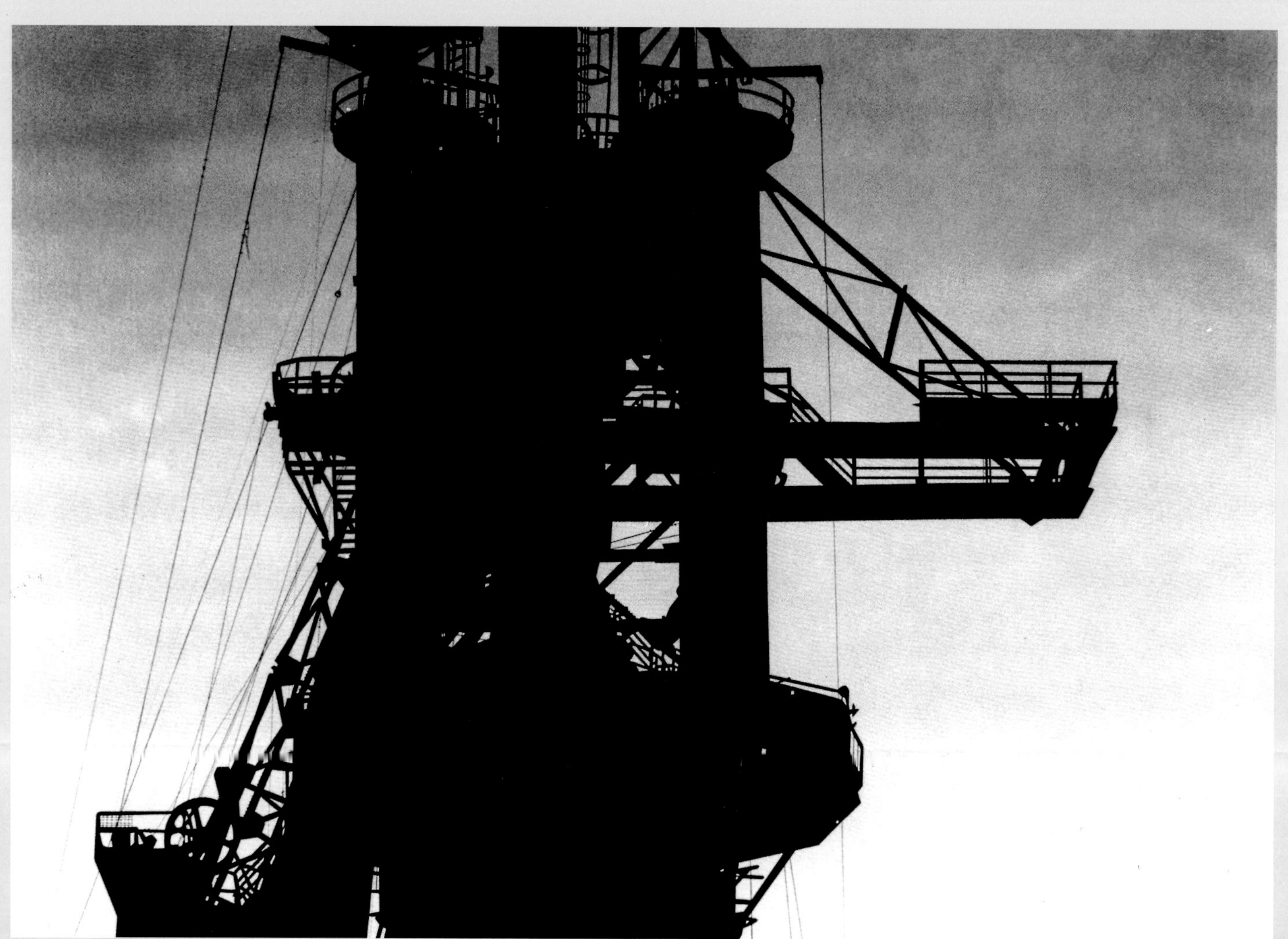

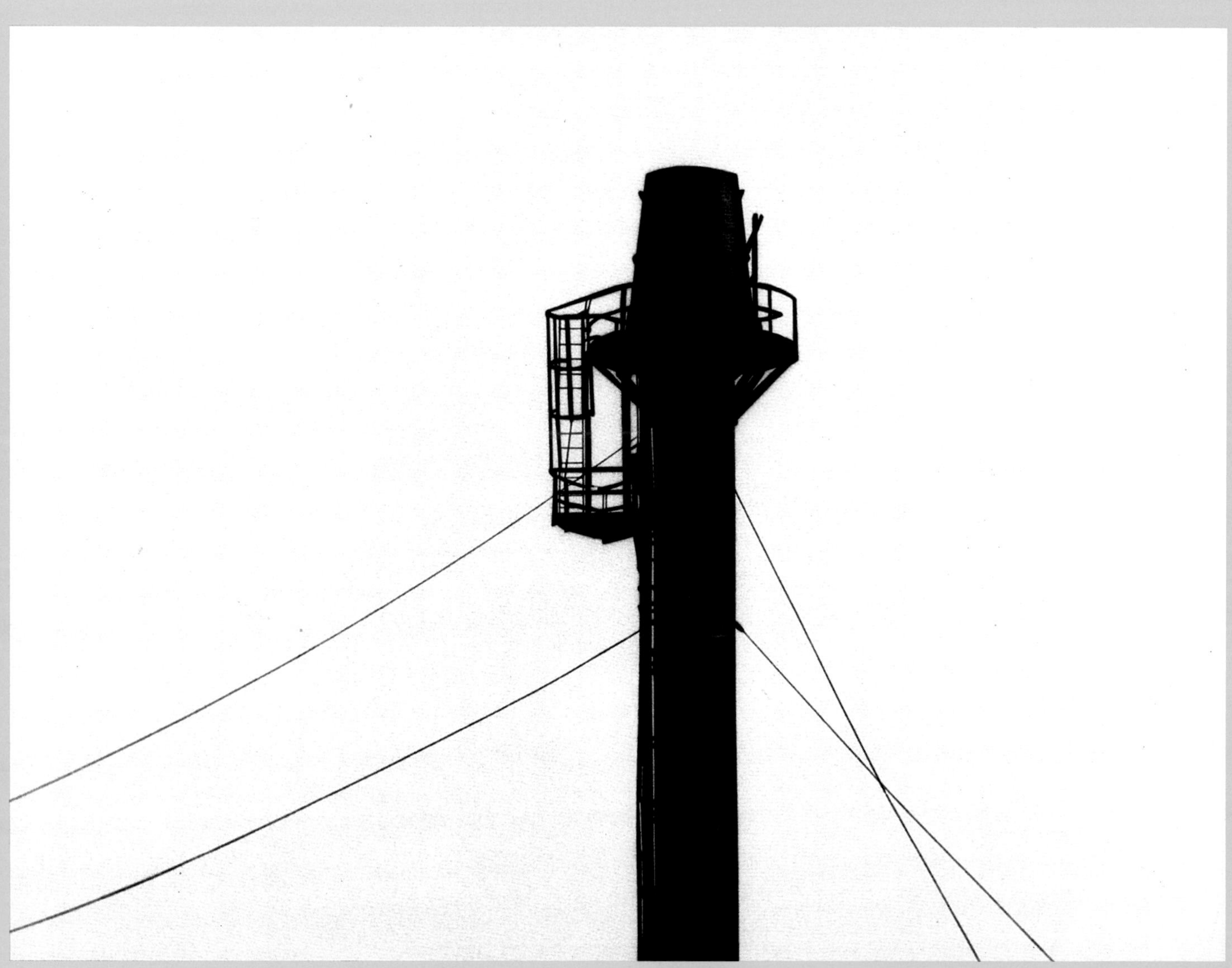

Title: *Stack*

Year: 1985

Medium: Watercolor

Size: 22" X 30"

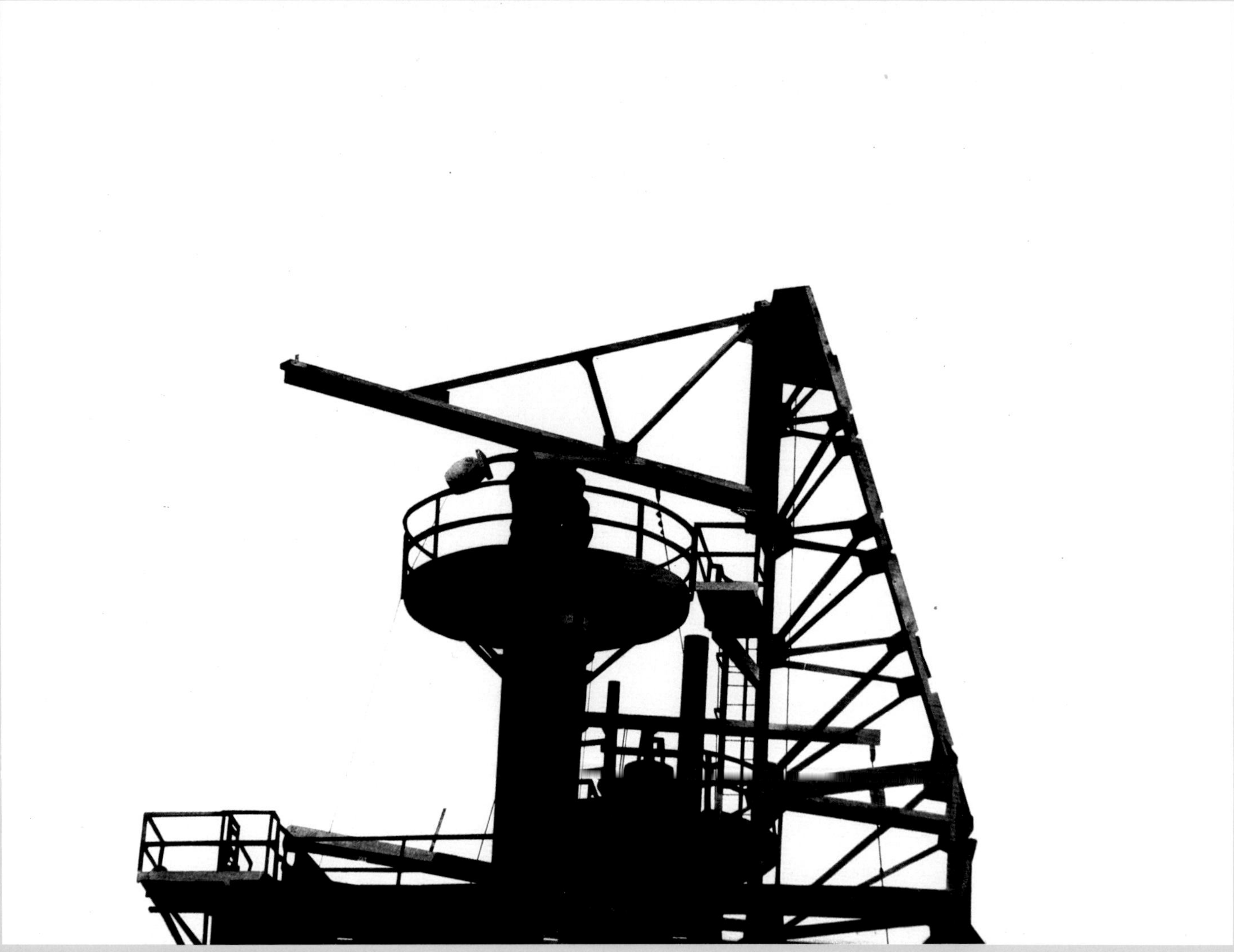

Title: *View from the Tracks*

Year: 1986

Medium: Watercolor

Size: 20" X 30"

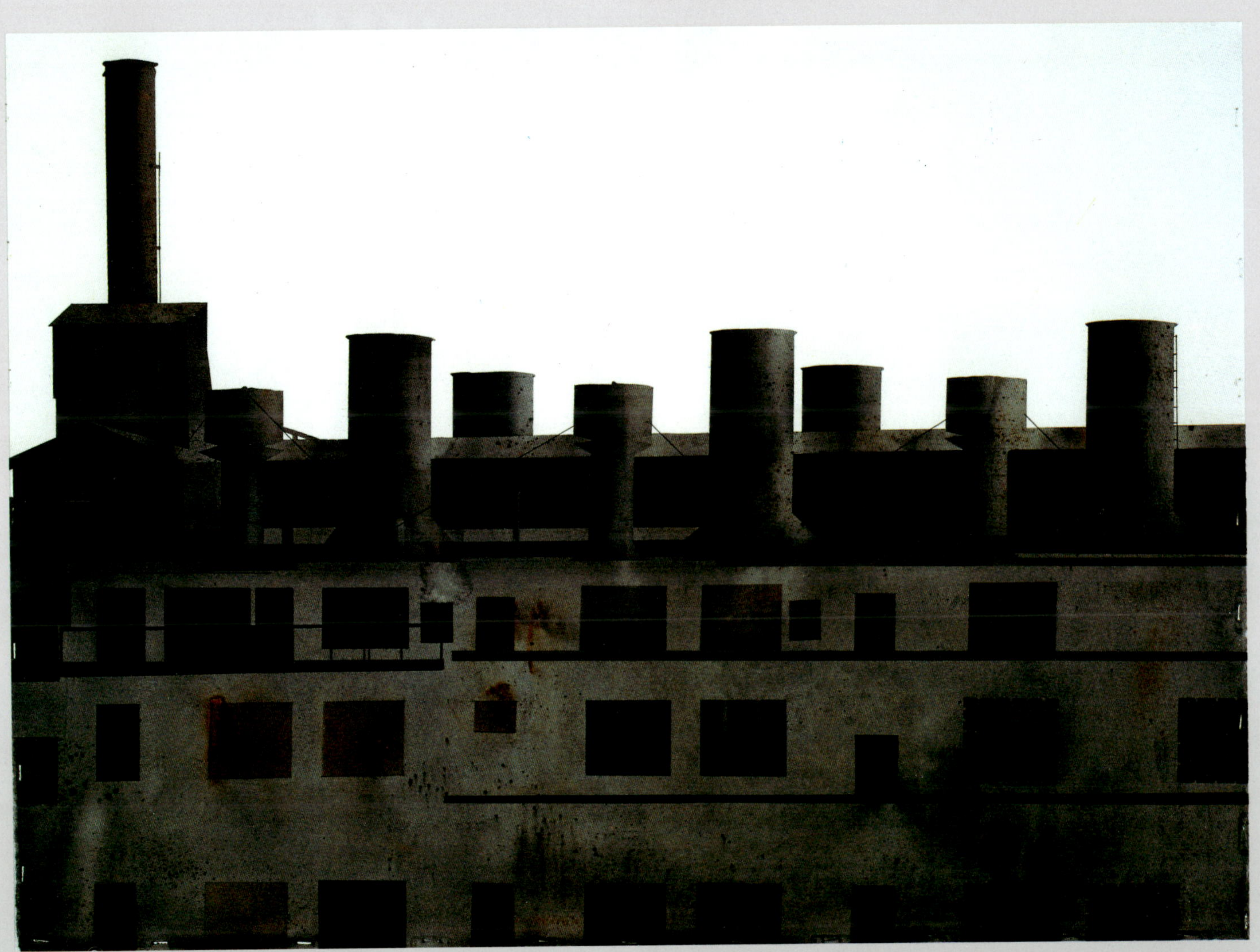

Title: *Steel Mill Wall*

Year: 1986

Medium: Watercolor

Size: 22" X 30"

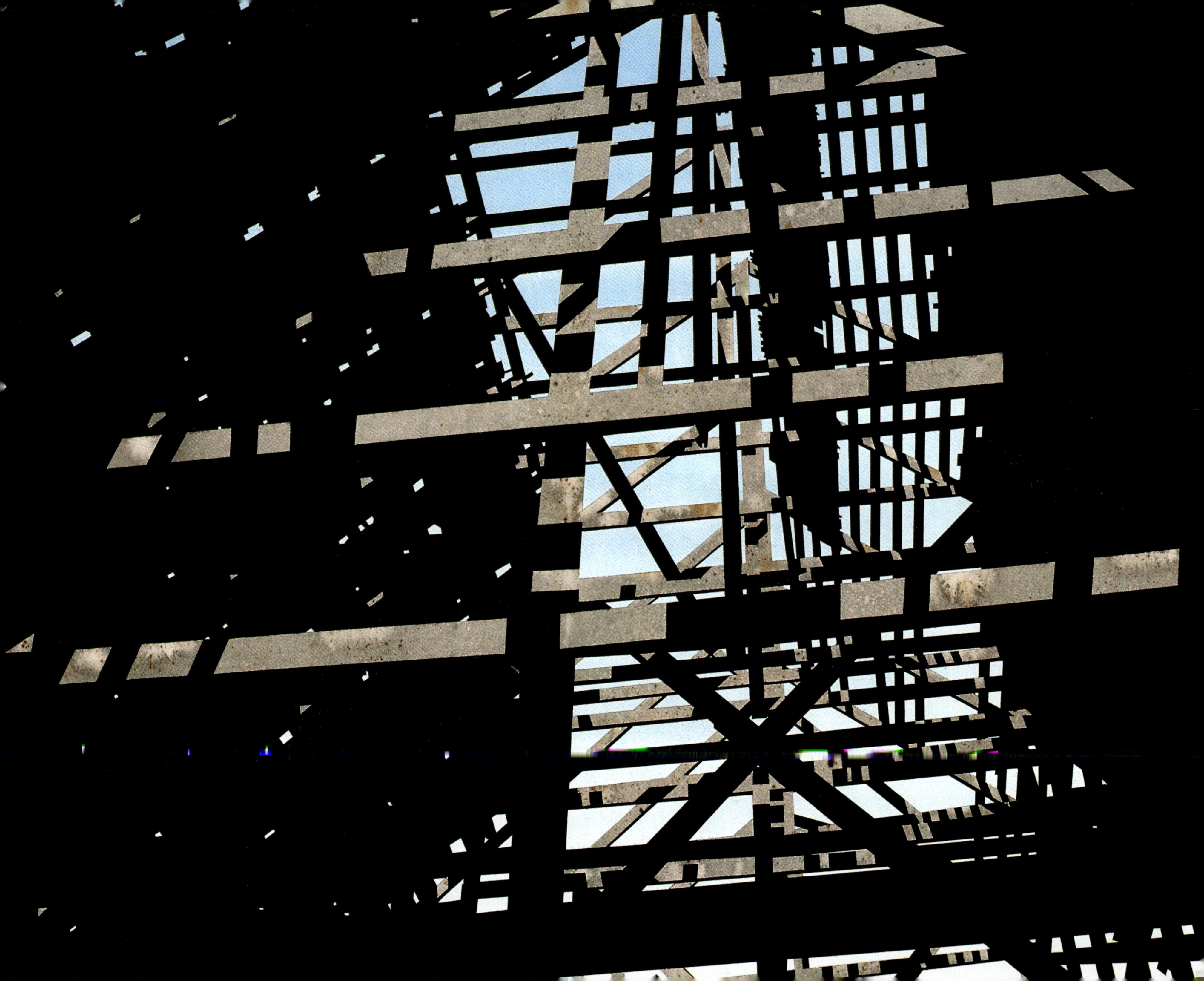

Series Four

Florida Tobacco Barns

1985 - 1988

Like the obsolete steel mills, the tobacco barns of North Florida and Georgia are endangered buildings. They appealed to that paradoxical element in Dombek's temperament which contradicts his belief in the insignificance of subject matter: his nostalgia for his roots in the vanishing landscape of the past. "I don't consider myself a romantic," he has insisted, "and I am not a documentary painter."[13] However in 1980 he took a job teaching architecture at Florida A & M University in Tallahassee, where he still lives, and the University gave him and his students a grant to study and record more than 500 abandoned tobacco barns. In these barns, he found a motif made to order for his dual if conflicting interest in abstract form and meaningful subject.

From a purely formal standpoint, these many "views" of timbered barns in various states of dilapidation are Dombek's best work. They combine the excitement of the tilted-back perspective and rhythmic diagonals of the fire escape series with the forceful interplay of silhouettes in the steel mill series, and they hark back to those Ozark barns which gave Dombek his beginning in art. What he started ten

Opposite page

Title: *Crosses*

Year: 1987

Medium: Watercolor

Size: 30" X 42"

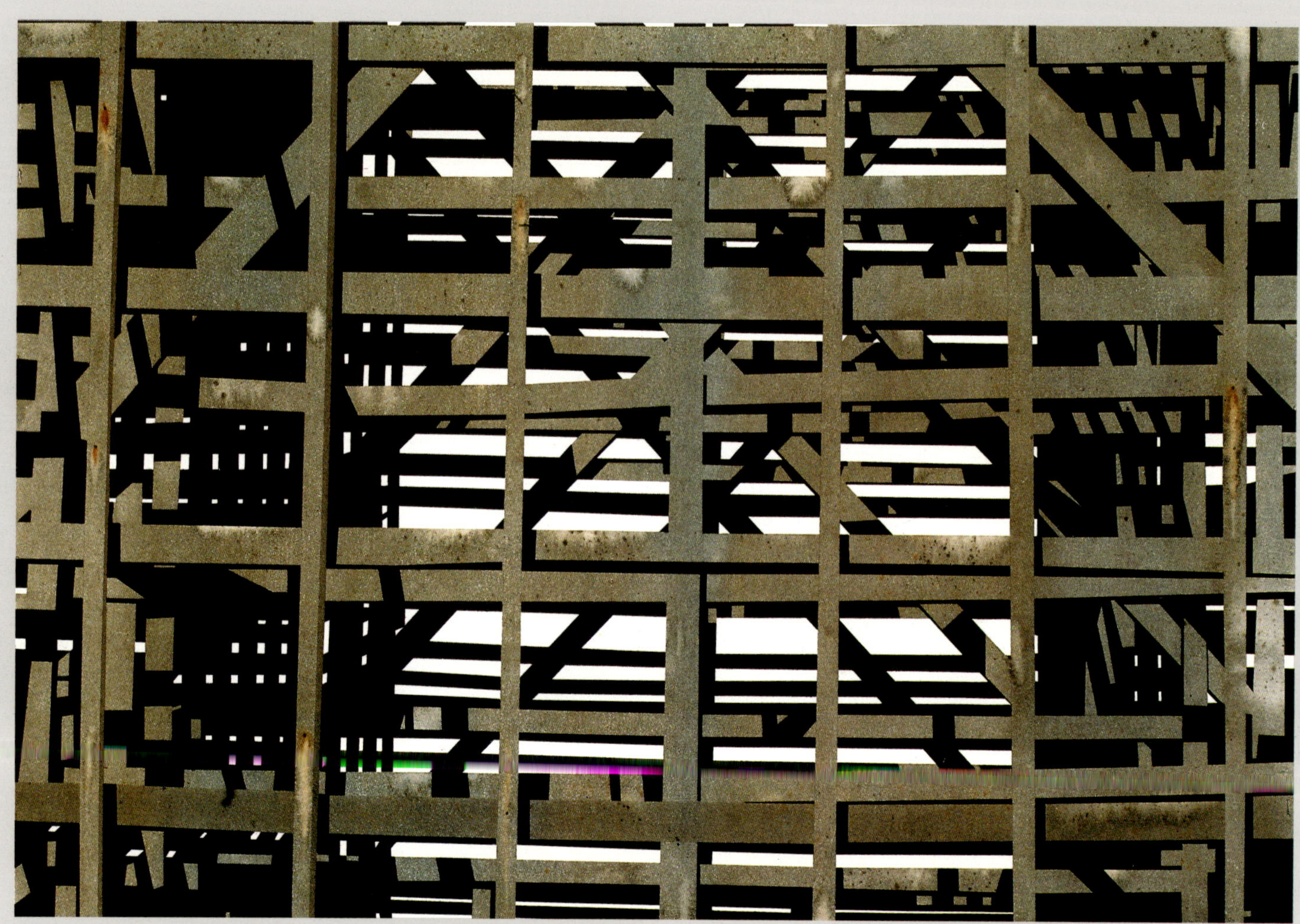

Title: *Wooden Rhythm*

Year: 1986

Medium: Watercolor

Size: 40" X 60"

years earlier by his discovery of the grid patterns in crates and hay barn timbers is now brought to fruition in this series of complex overlapping perspectives. "You might say that I build a painting as much as I paint a painting," this architect-painter has said.[14] These tobacco barn pictures are truly constructions, which awe the eye with their visual "carpentry."

The compositional importance of cropping, downplayed in the steel mill series but essential to Dombek's scheme of spatial illusion, is here brought to the forefront, as Dombek moves, from picture to picture, either close to a depth-defying grid of timbers or back to a tilted-up perspective of roof beams. The possible combinations are endless, and Dombek threw all of his energies into it. "At one point during the two and a half years that I worked on this series," he recalls, "I worked 67 days straight without a break, from eight to 14 hours a day."[15] He adds, "Such a love affair developed that if not for Hurricane Kate which destroyed the barn I was working from, I might have continued this series for a number of years."

The years of "barn painting" were interspersed

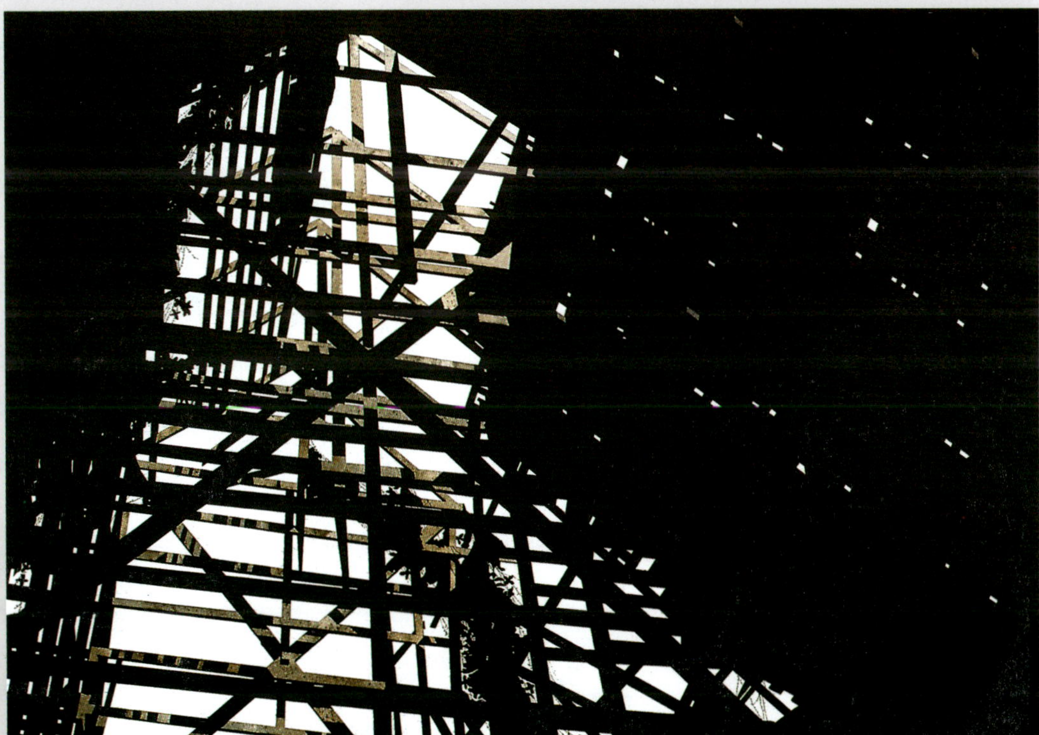

Title: *In the Light*

Year: 1987

Medium: Watercolor

Size: 30" X 42"

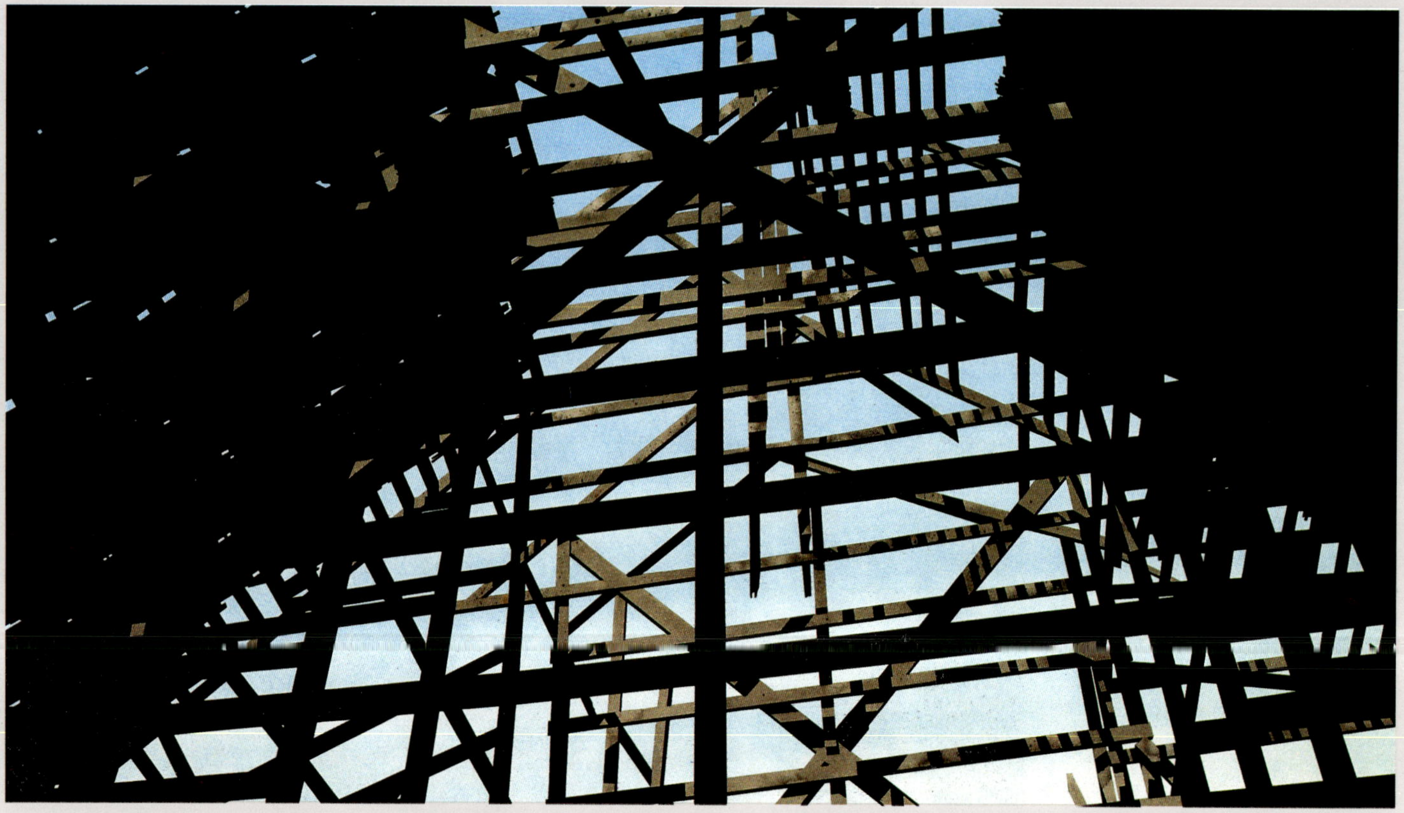

Title: *Tobacco Barn*

Year: 1987

Medium: Watercolor

Size: 40" X 60"

with a curious subject — one might call it his Scaffolding Series — that seems almost an aberration in the body of Dombek's work: a series of paintings devoted to the renovation of the Tallahassee Jail, an Art Deco architectural oddity. Dombek sought to relieve the severity of his geometry in the scaffolding the workmen were using with the palmetto designs of the quaint Art Deco panels in etched glass. The combination of organic forms clashing with rigid geometry reminds the viewer of Louis Sullivan's architecture. One of this series, *On a Clear Day*, 1987, was selected to adorn the cover of the catalog for Dombek's 1988 retrospective at the Butler Institute. The combination of creamy facade with timbered scaffolding recalls an earlier Dombek experiment, the *South of Damman—North of al Khobar*. *South of Damman* was painted in 1982 while Dombek was in Saudi Arabia on a one-year appointment in architecture at King Faisal University, a year of bad experiences resulting in some not-like-Dombek pictures, such as the *South of Damman*, which has a dominant human figure, a workman seen

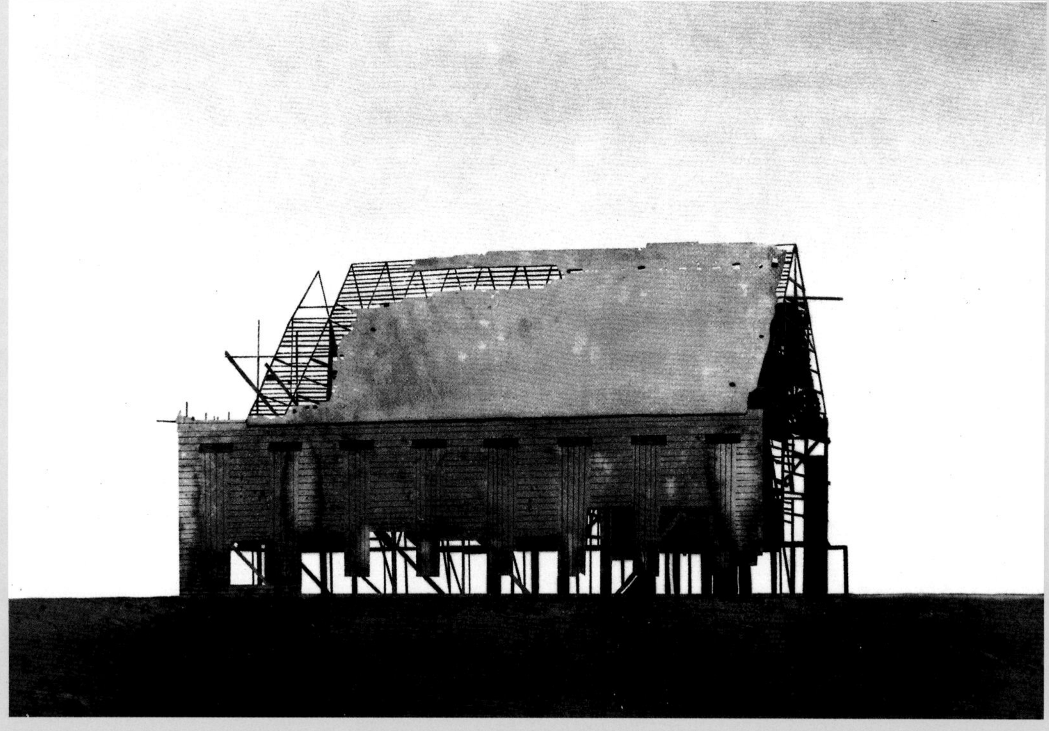

Title: *Barn on a Plain*

Year: 1986

Medium: Watercolor

Size: 30" X 42"

from the back walking through a doorway surrounded by a rickety scaffold.

But the Arabian scaffolds came before the Tallahassee jail scaffolds, and both together prefigure and anticipate the scaffold-like patterns of the Tobacco Barn series. A scaffold, whether a workman's platform or an executioner's, is a temporary thing. Whether or not Dombek was consciously aware of it, his art makes permanent the temporary. Hence his interest in decaying barns, and hence his choice of a fugitive medium, watercolor, to which he can devote enormous quantities of time and patience. One learns that the very word "scaffold" derives from an Old French word, *eschace*, meaning "tilt"; most of these pictures are characterized by the tilting diagonals that go back to those Ozark vegetable crates and constitute the dominant compositional and rhythmic device of Dombek's art...until he abandoned it for the sake of his rock paintings. ■

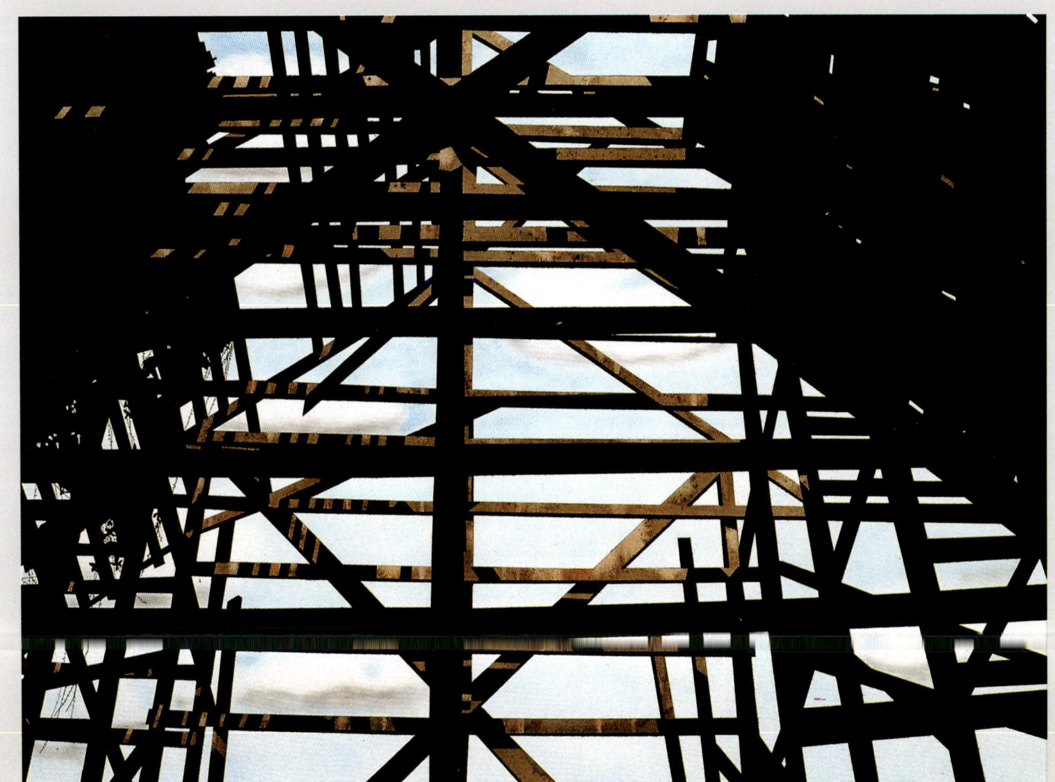

Title: *Barn Near Havana*

Year: 1987

Medium: Watercolor

Size: 30" X 42"

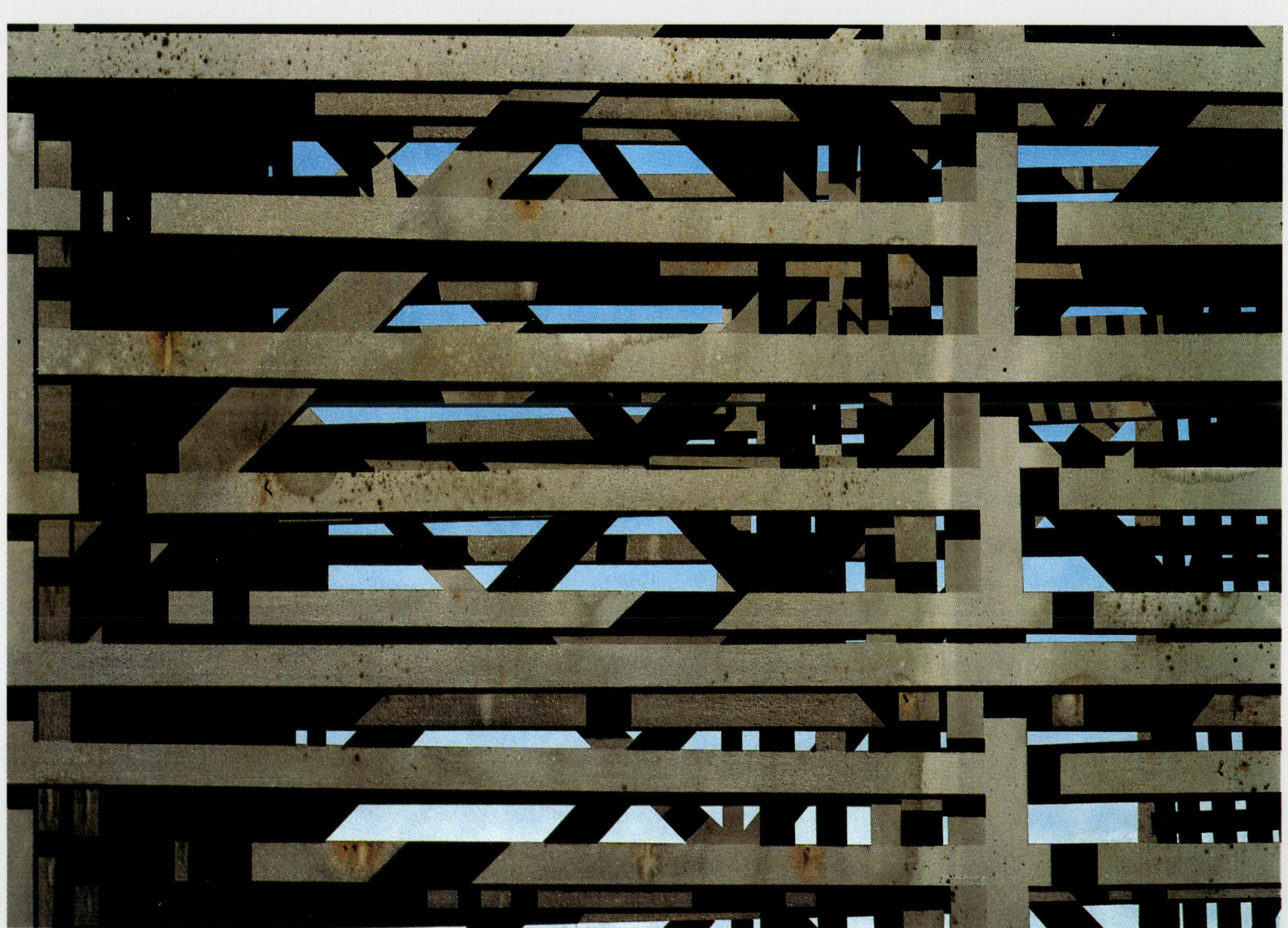

Title: *Blue Grid*

Year: 1986

Medium: Watercolor

Size: 30" X 42"

Title: *Inside the Barn*

Year: 1987

Medium: Watercolor

Size: 40" X 60"

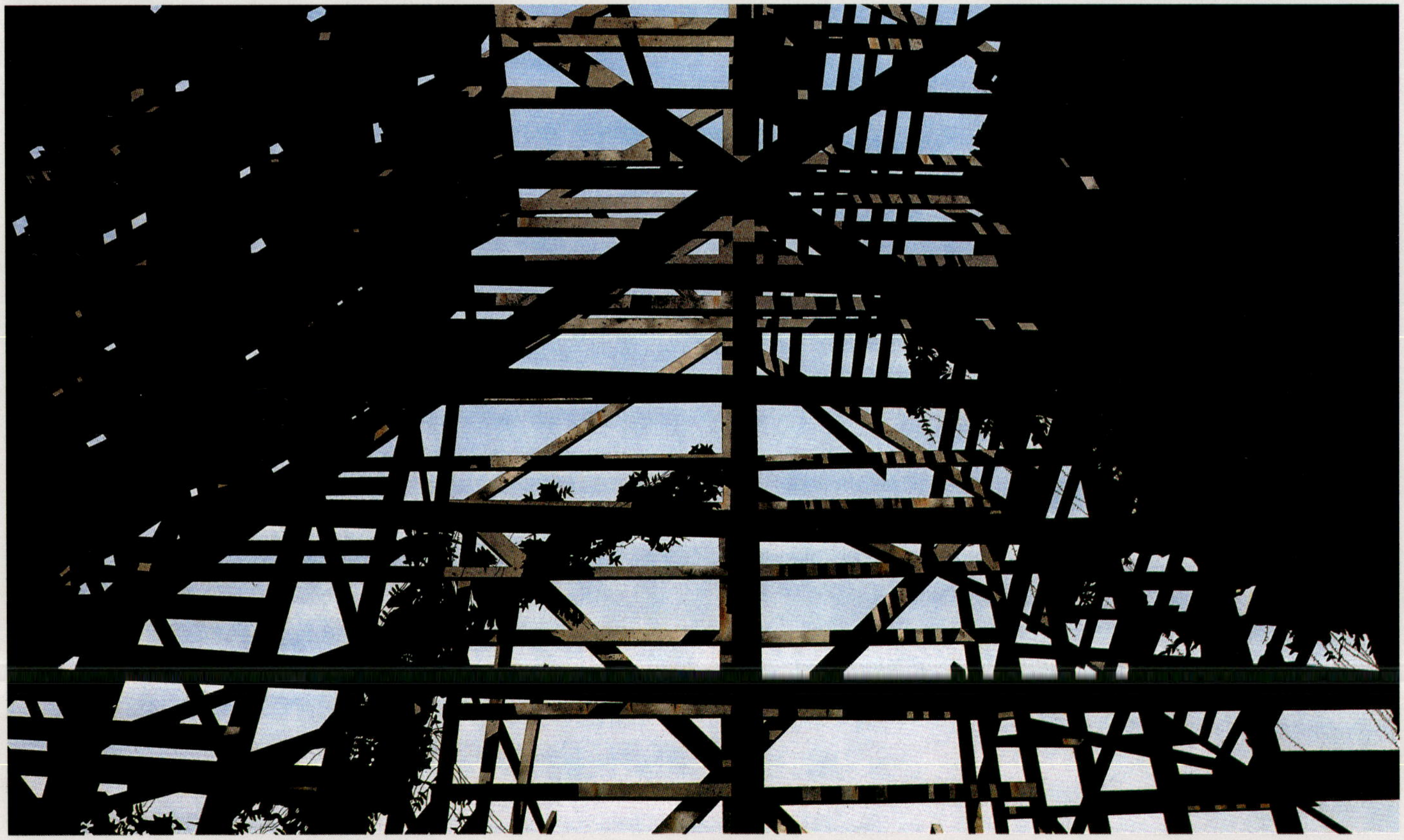

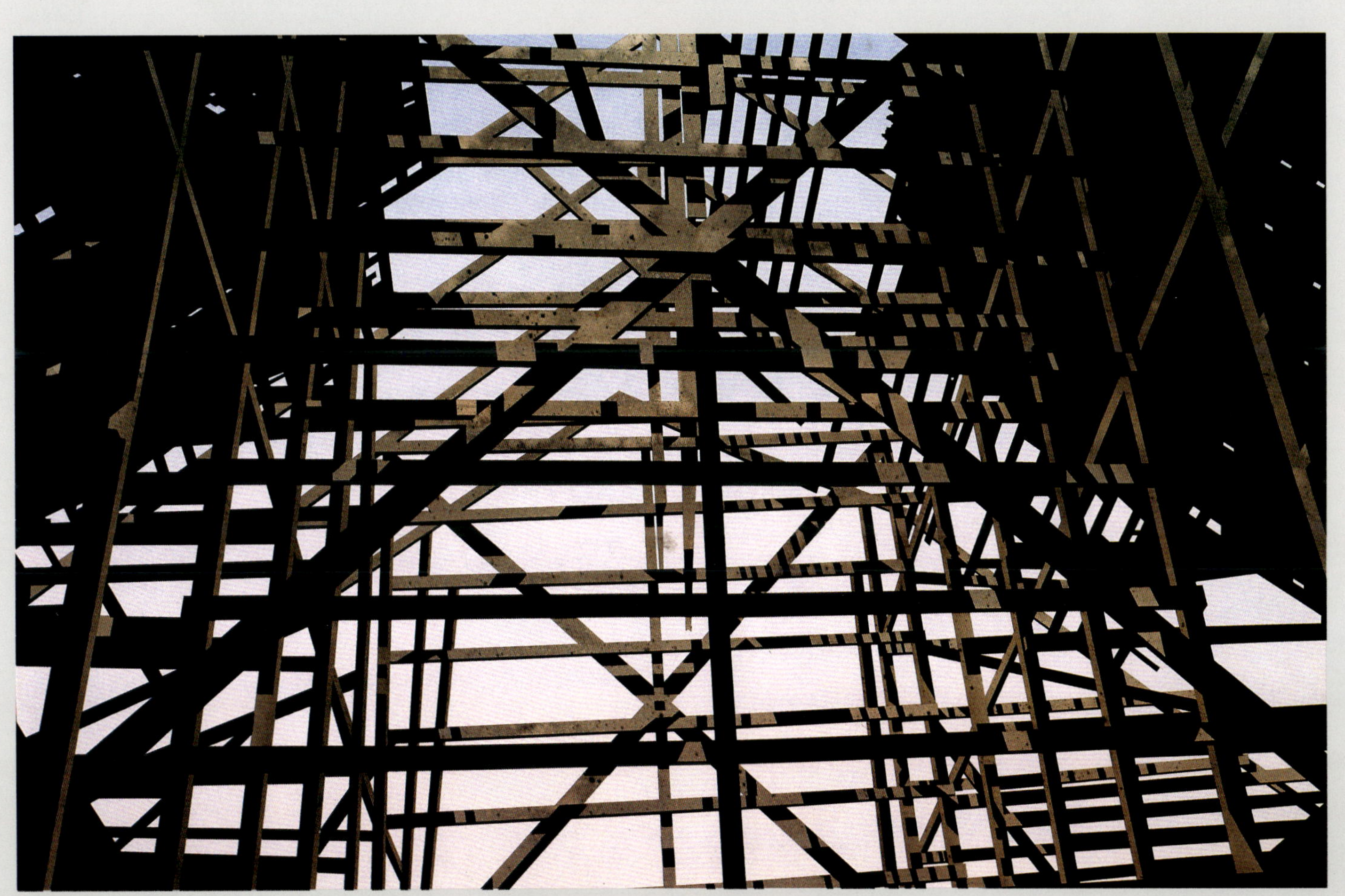

Title: *Barn*

Year: 1987

Medium: Watercolor

Size: 40" X 60"

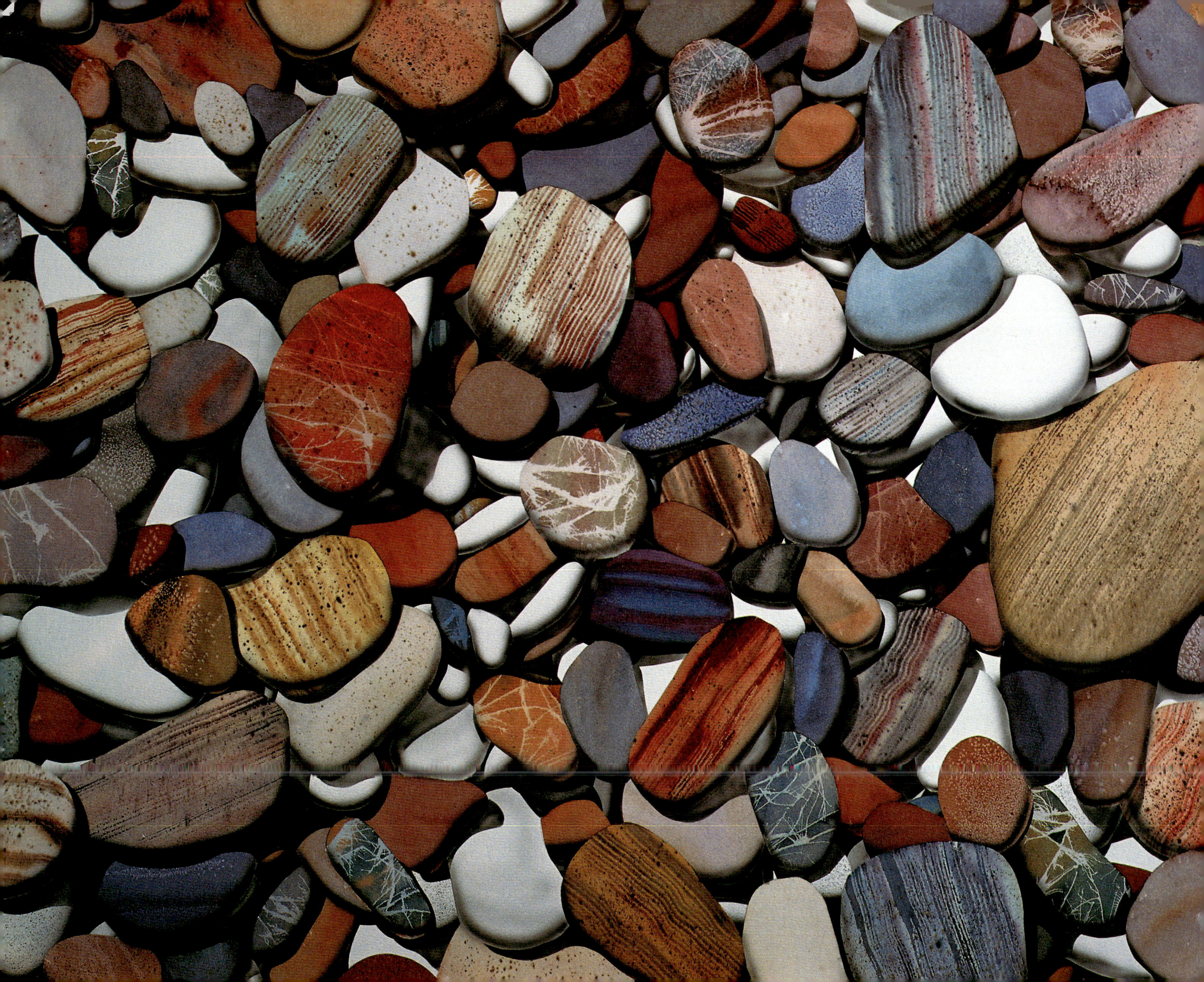

Series Five

Rocks

1989 - 1994

After the major retrospective of his work in the summer of 1988 at the Butler Institute, Dombek accepted a one-year teaching position in Florence, Italy, hoping to receive motivation for a new direction in his work. "I have always received inspiration by moving to a new area and being stimulated visually," he has said.[16] On the island of Elba, Dombek was captivated by the white beaches littered with millions of jewel-like marble stones polished smooth and shiny by eons of tidal abrasion. Making his first watercolor painting of them, just as they lay, scattered by chance and tides and gleaming in the Mediterranean sunlight, Dombek realized a subject ideally suited to the nature of his medium. This subject with all of its curves and colors, broke dramatically with the constructive angular series he had been painting for years.

Before leaving Elba, he gathered up from the beaches as many of those rocks as he could cram into his suitcases, and took them back to Florida, where he could reconstruct in his studio the beach habitat of the rocks, and paint directly from the rocks instead of using photographs. Accustomed to painting the same subject repeatedly, not even he could realize that he would spend five years of his life capturing these rocks in more than 200 separate paintings.

Opposite page

Title: *Lake Michigan Rocks*

Year: 1994

Medium: Watercolor

Size: 30" X 42"

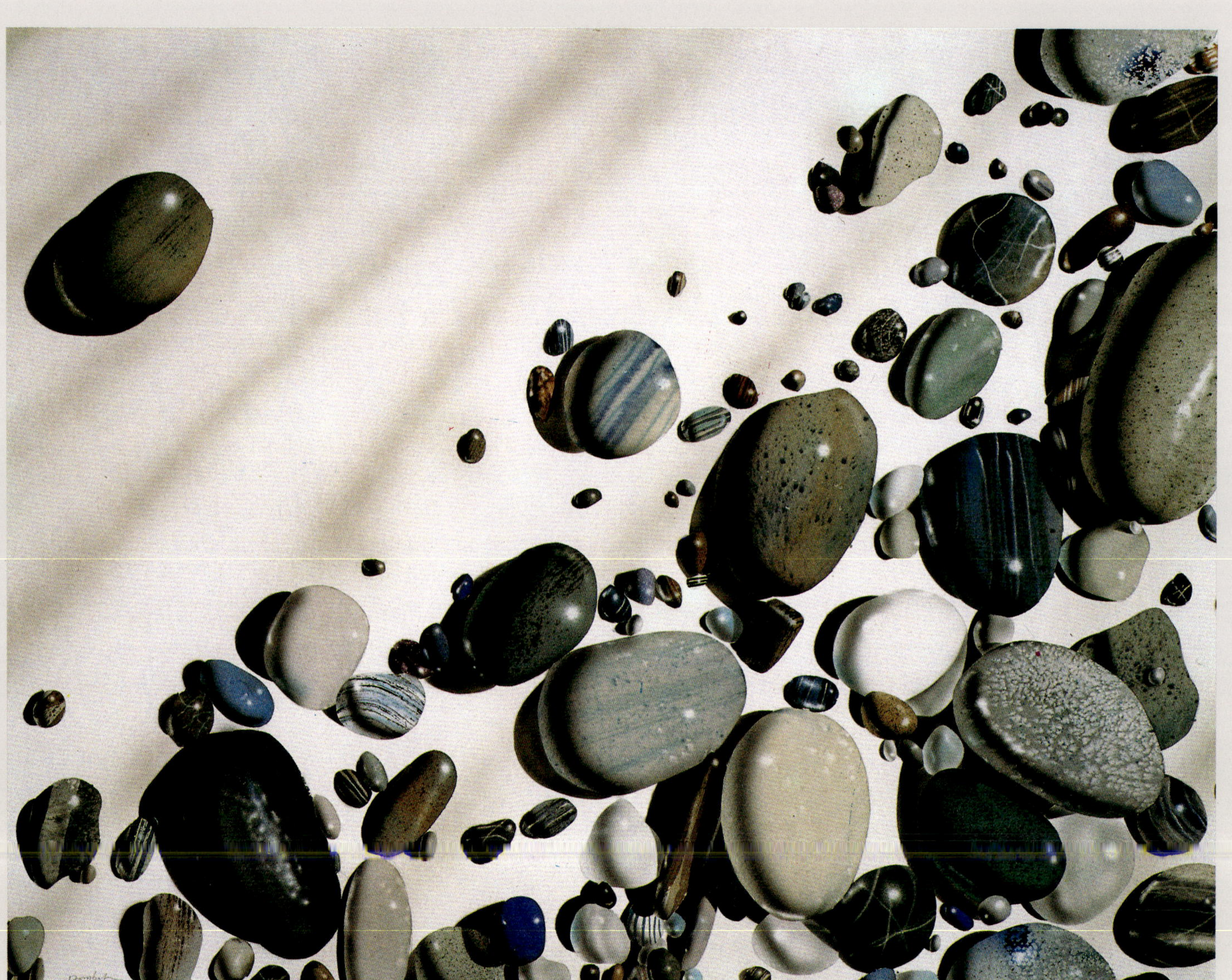

Title: *White & Blue Rocks*

Year: 1993

Medium: Watercolor

Size: 22" X 30"

If this is monomania, a strong case may be made for the fact that no two of these rock paintings are alike, and Dombek sensed, early on, what great potential this subject offered for formal investigation and modification. The nuances of composition, color, light (and reflected light) began to make Dombek understand what pattern means: not just an arbitrary design imposed by man but an inherent event in nature. Making order out of chaos had been his motive all along, and now, in the arrangement and rearrangement of these stones, he found his most cooperative "models." He could be challenged to make these rocks lie in the sand as he had found them, to lie there in "random" order that was more orderly than random. The rock paintings also have given Dombek a perfect means of continuing his play with what deserves to be named after him the "Dombek Paradox": the controlled use of spontaneity, the manipulation of accident, or the "planned chance," as he has called it.[17] Going back to that White Series of vegetable crates which he

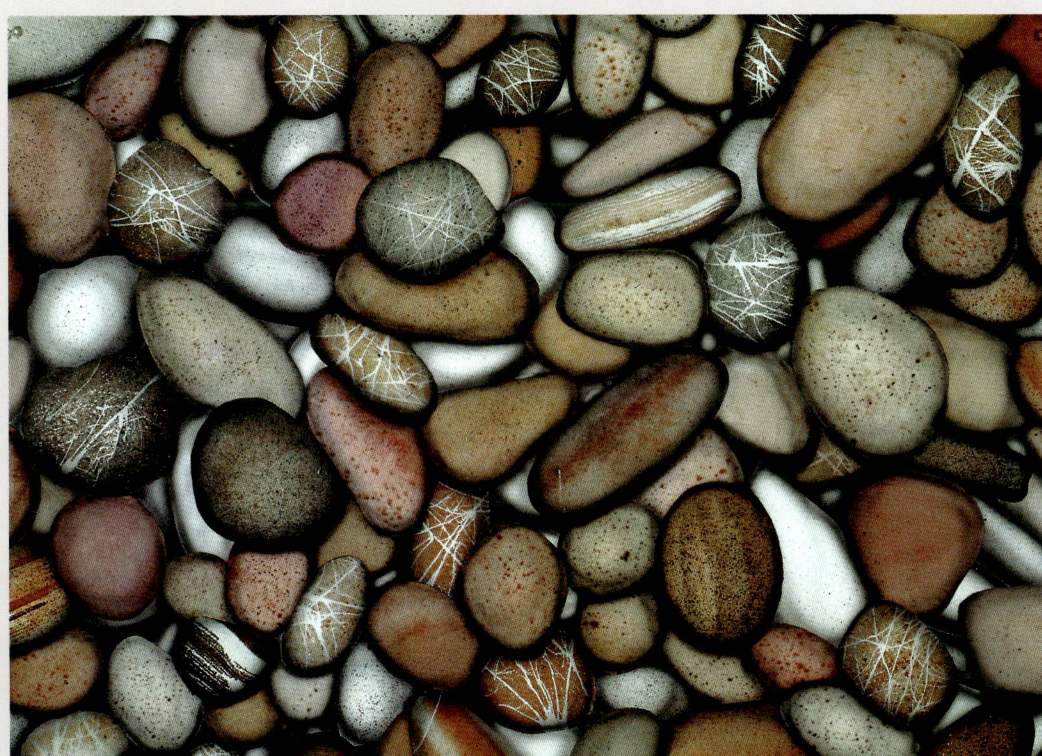

Title: *Fish Creek*

Year: 1994

Medium: Watercolor

Size: 22" X 30"

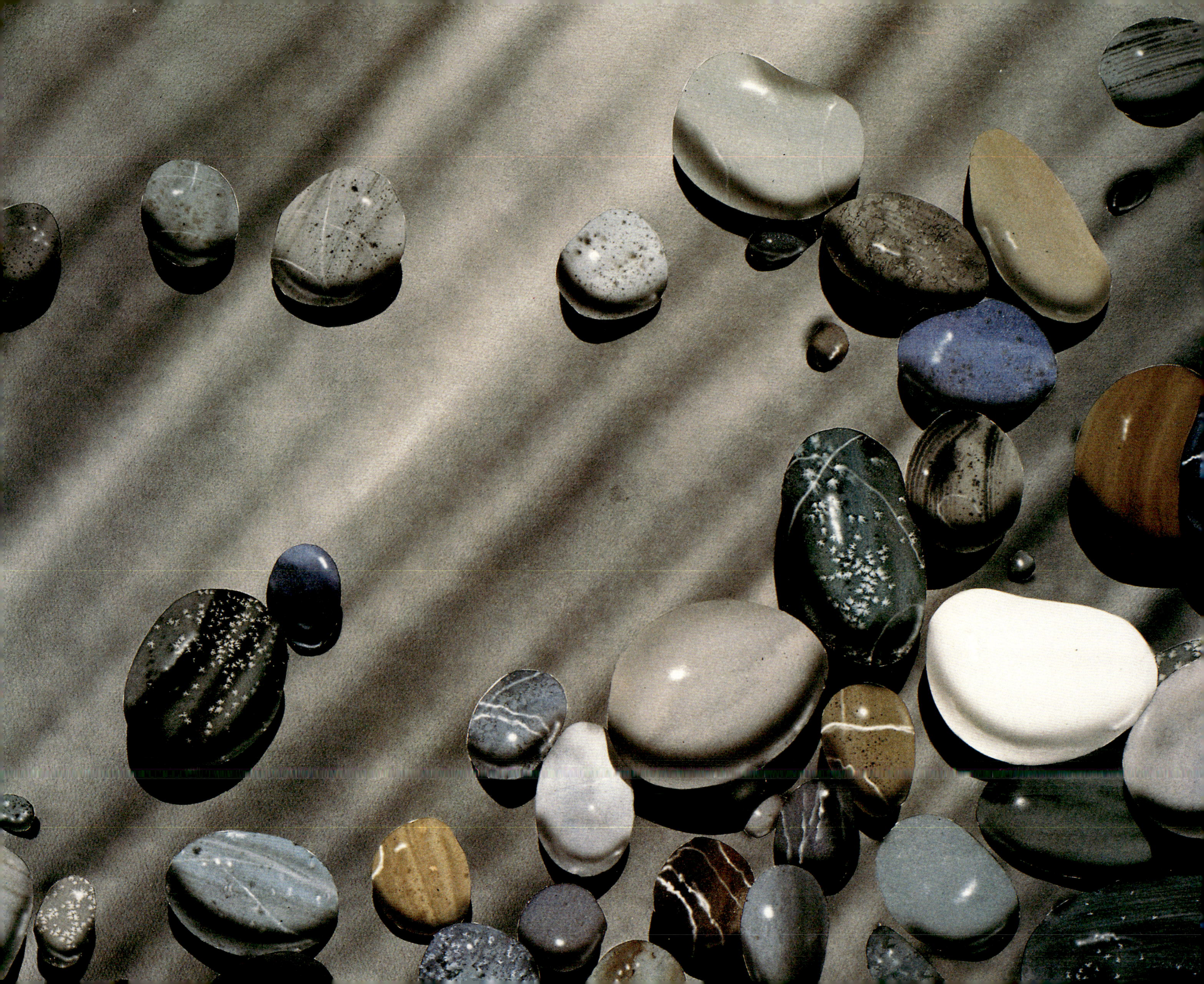

executed as a student, there have always been areas in a Dombek watercolor which seem to have been left to chance — the critic Alfred Frankenstein refers to this as "puddling."[18] These are spots where Dombek has allowed watercolor to be what it naturally wants to be: fluid, runny, and apparently casual. Actually Dombek has never allowed the medium to assert its will over his own will; like a horse-tamer he has given the beast the belief that it has not surrendered its true nature, so long as it is agreeable to obeying him. The result has been a happy utilization of the strength of the freedom of serendipitous strokes in order to complement the rigid control that is his trademark.

In the rock pictures, then, not only has Dombek randomly arranged the patterns of the rocks, but he has also been able to enjoy all the beauty of spontaneity in the application of the paint itself. No wonder that he has never grown restless or bored in his long "rock period."

The rock pictures are Dombek's most popular work. "I've met the rock people," he has noted. "There are people out there who love rocks. They carry them around with them. During shows of these paintings, people would pull me aside to show me their favorite rock. I've also learned which parts of the world have the best rocks, because these people know."[19]

Possibly one reason for the popularity of

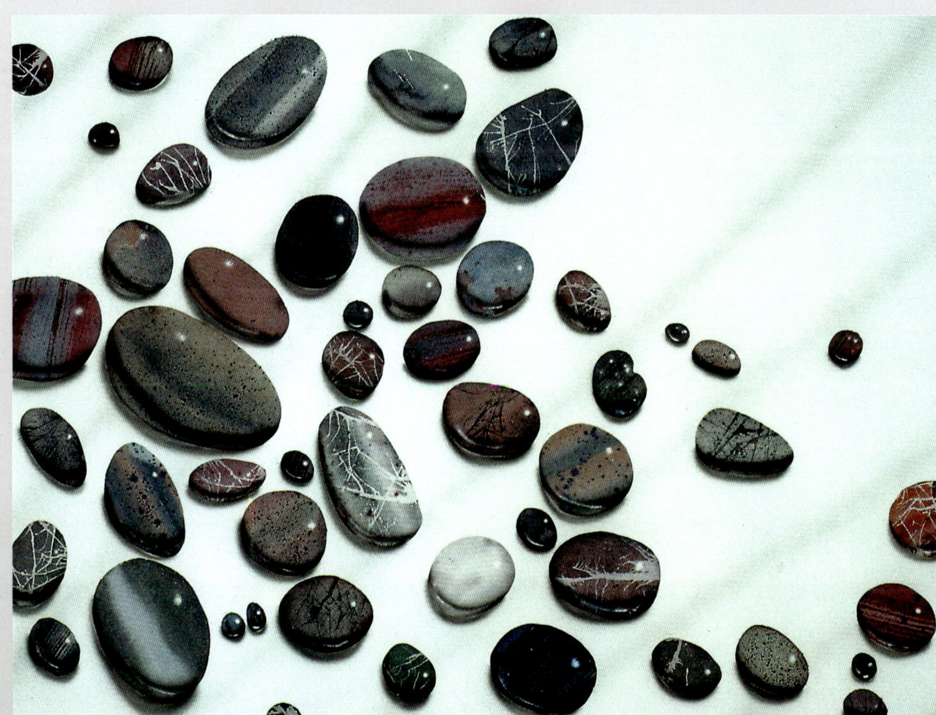

Opposite page

Title: *White Rock*

Year: 1990

Medium: Watercolor

Size: 22" X 30"

Title: *Marble Rocks*

Year: 1994

Medium: Watercolor

Size: 22" X 30"

Dombek's rock pictures is that of all his truly realistic paintings, they are the most "real." Ironically, since these are the paintings that he has done directly from the objects, not from his photographs, Dombek's rock pictures have been complimented for looking most like photographs. This somewhat bothers him, and he says, "I think people who say this are not looking at photographs or paintings in an intense way." The so-called photorealists are so exact in their replication of photographs that they paint some areas out of focus. [20]

This is not a Dombek painting of the rocks at Elba but a Dombek photograph of the beach at Elba, from which he gathered the rocks he would incorporate into so many of his paintings. A cursory comparison of the photograph and any Dombek painting of the rocks reveals at once the main differences: parts of the photograph are slightly out of focus, and Dombek has seldom duplicated that photographic quality. Few of Dombek's paintings are as packed with such a multitude of stones; the rocks completely cover and obscure the white sand beneath them. There are "extraneous" objects, sticks and such, littering

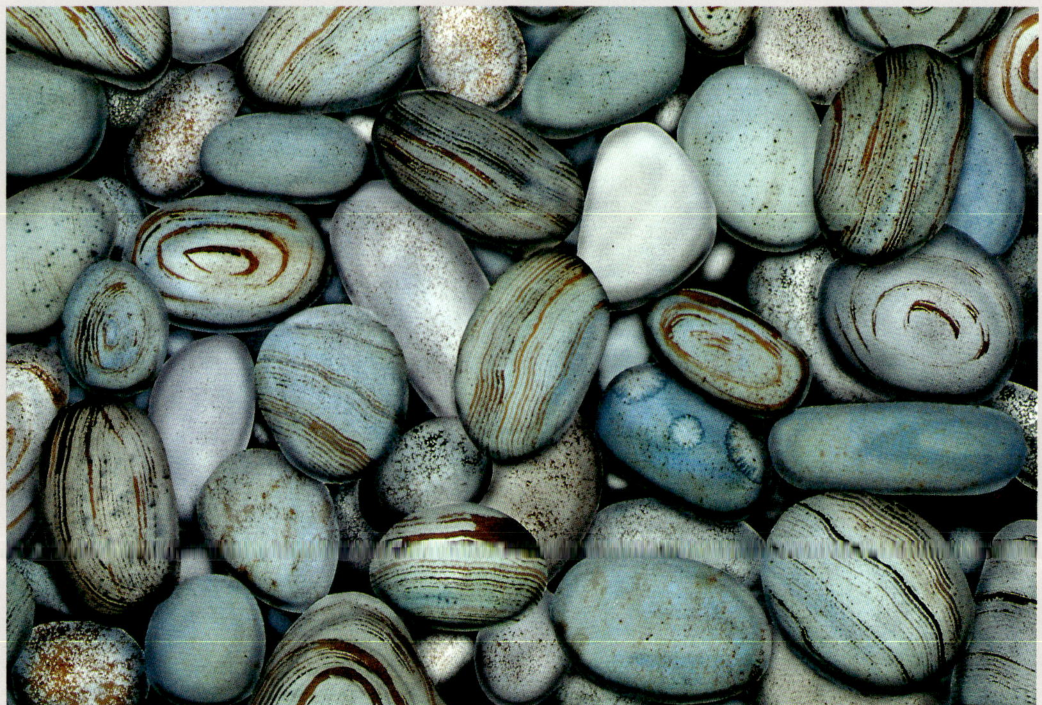

Title: *Alberta*

Year: 1994

Medium: Watercolor

Size: 22" X 30"

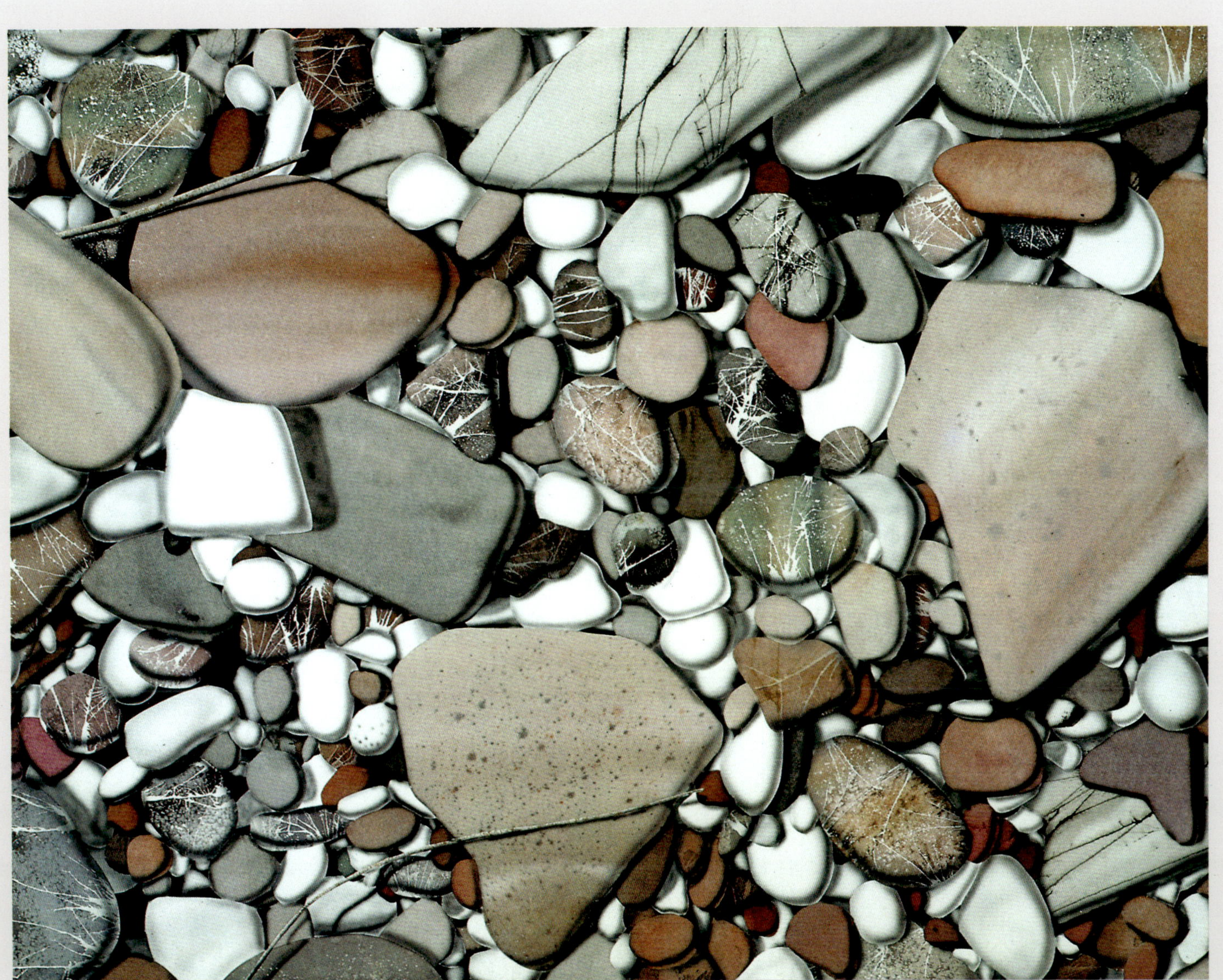

Title: *North Port*

Year: 1993

Medium: Watercolor

Size: 22" X 30"

the picture; and the angle of perspective is the "natural" view of the camera looking down a shoreline, not the "composed" angle of the artist's eye, which usually sees the rocks directly from above. The picture looks photorealistic because it is a photograph; Dombek's paintings are not.

They are paintings, and the viewer who studies them will perceive how they differ from photographs. Despite the detail which faithfully renders the actual appearance of objects, they are not the chemical emulsions of photographic processes but pigments of paint with the nature of paint, specifically fluid watercolor. The highlights which seem to glisten on the surface of the stones are, as any true white in watercolor must be, simply blank white paper, unpainted; and the spaces between stones, also mostly white paper, are the real substance of the composition, organized in their randomness like a game of Go, with infinite mathematical

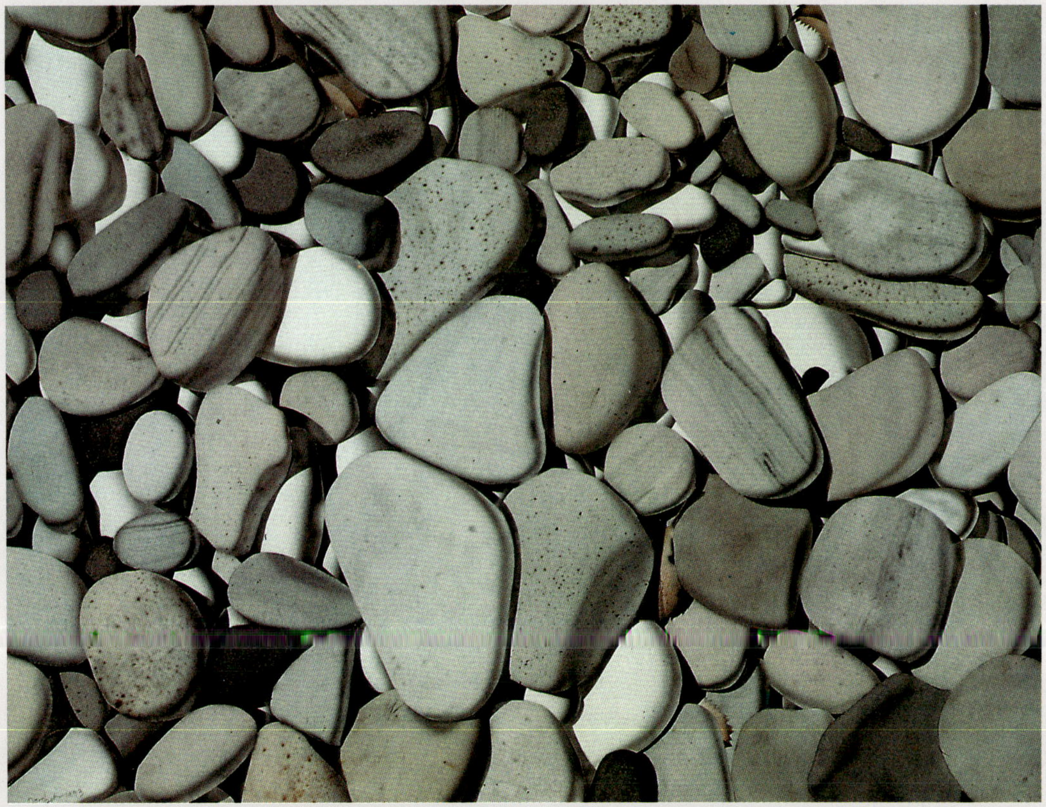

Title: *Rocks of Lake Michigan*

Year: 1994

Medium: Watercolor

Size: 22" X 30"

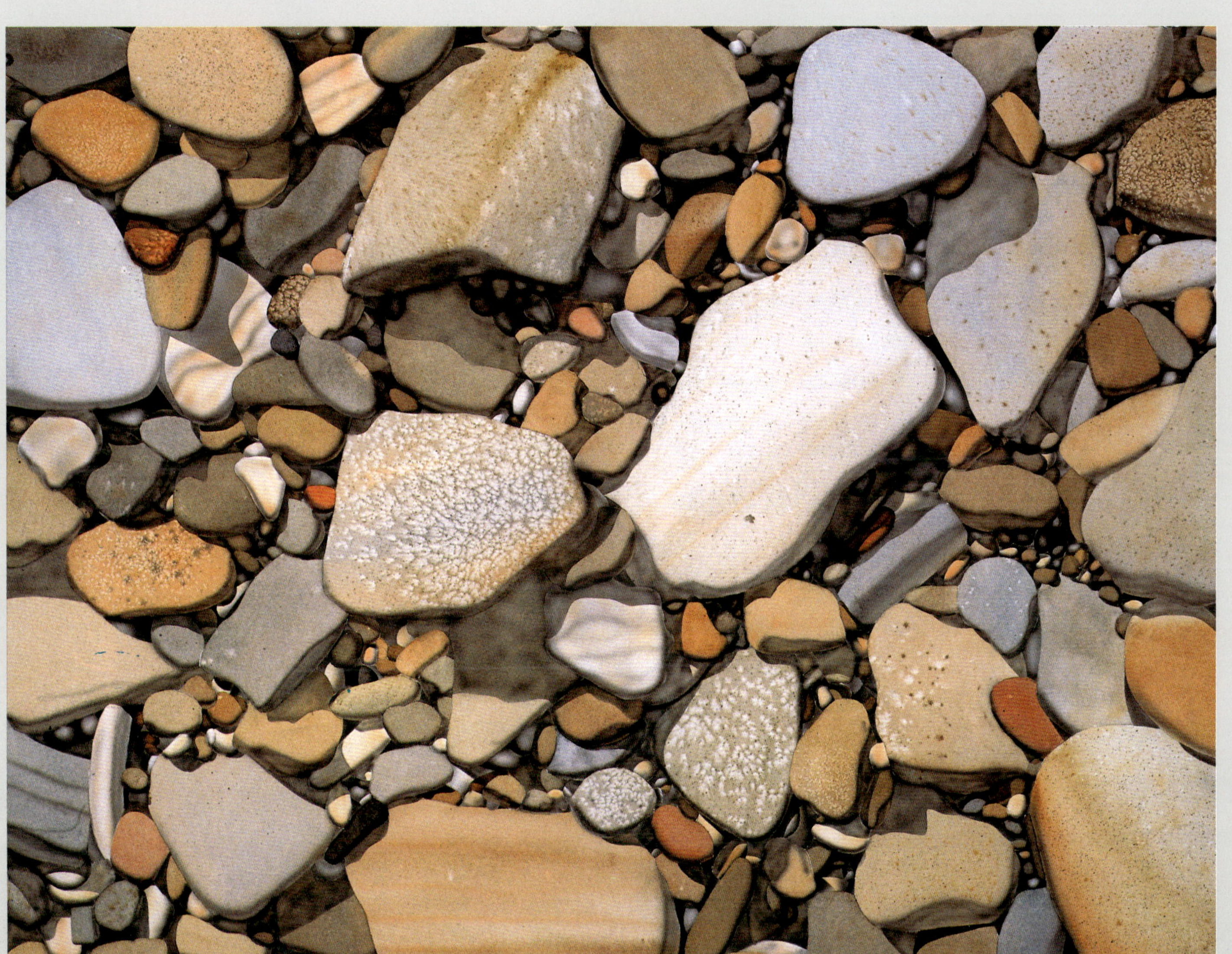

Title: *Mulberry River*

Year: 1994

Medium: Watercolor

Size: 22" X 30"

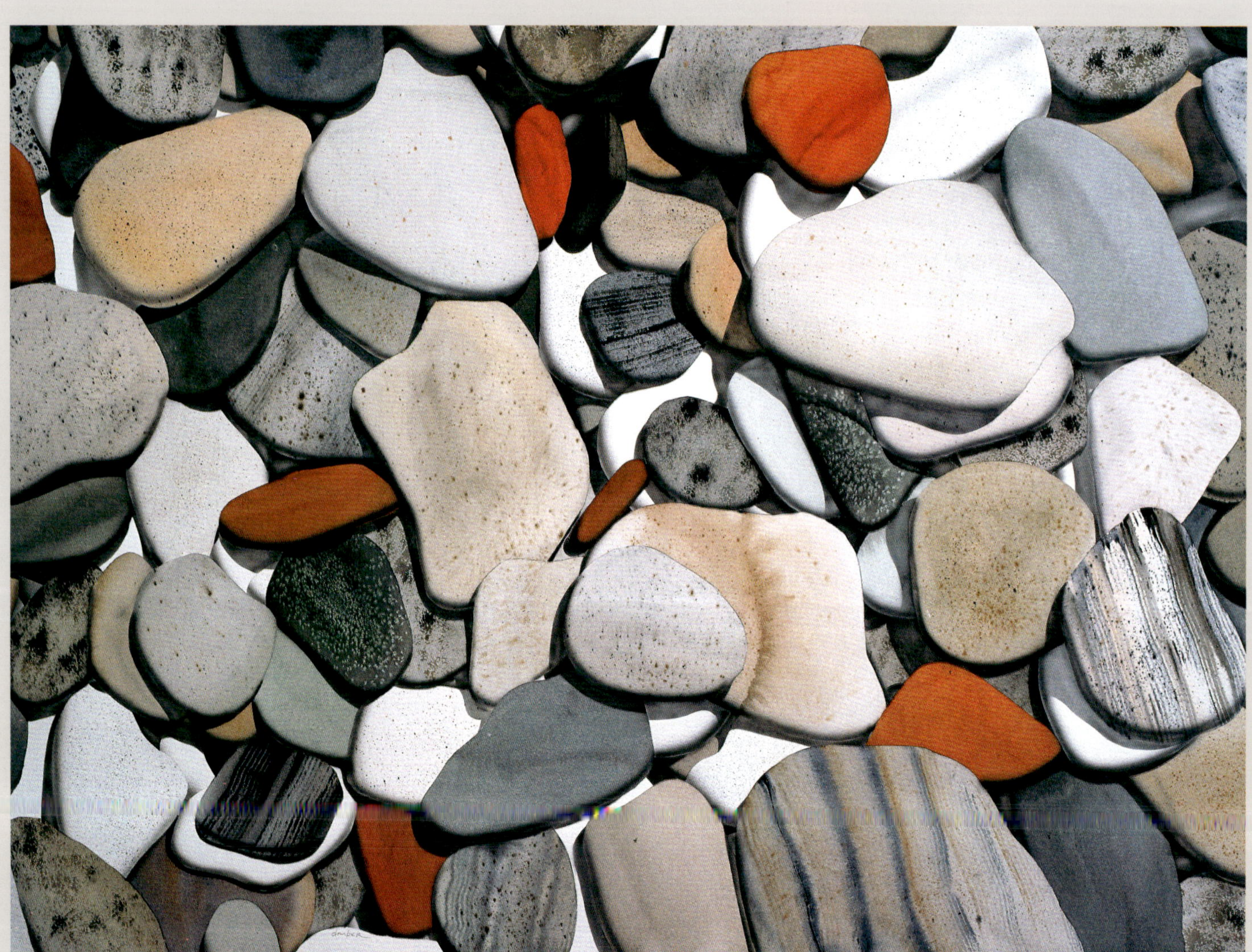

Title: *Seven Red Rocks*

Year: 1994

Medium: Watercolor

Size: 30" x 42"

"meaning."

If one must find a "message" in these paintings, in order to ward off the feeling that they are only decorative, then all one has to do is to consider that in many of them one of the stones may rest apart from the others, isolated, outcast, reclusive, speaking volumes about the position of the individual in a society of kindred but different souls.

These are Dombek's self-portraits, to the extent that he has ever done them or will ever do them. He intends, he says, to paint this subject matter for a long time — not just the rocks of Elba but ones from the shores of Lake Michigan and the banks of the Buffalo River in his native Arkansas...where he hopes to return, for good. ■

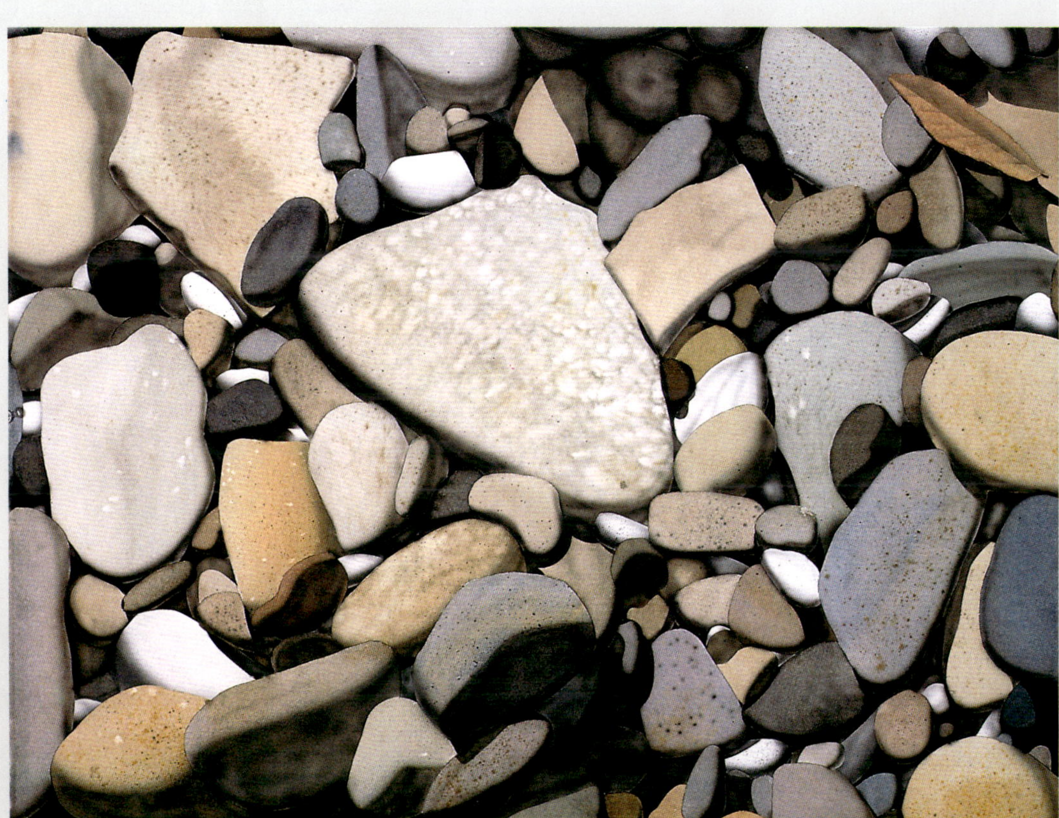

Title: *Turner's Bend*

Year: 1994

Medium: Watercolor

Size: 22" X 30"

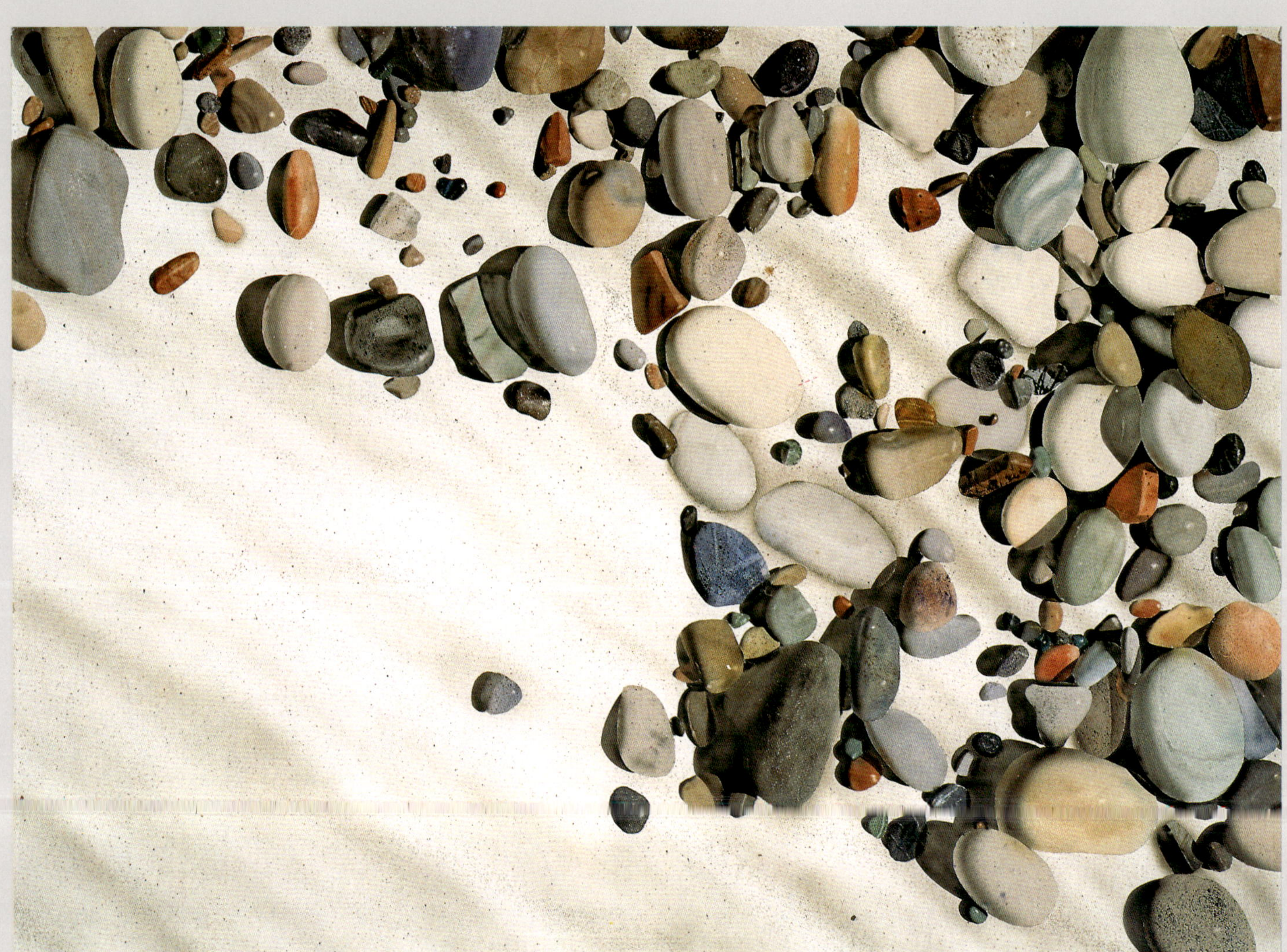

Title: *Gems*

Year: 1993

Medium: Watercolor

Size: 30" x 42"

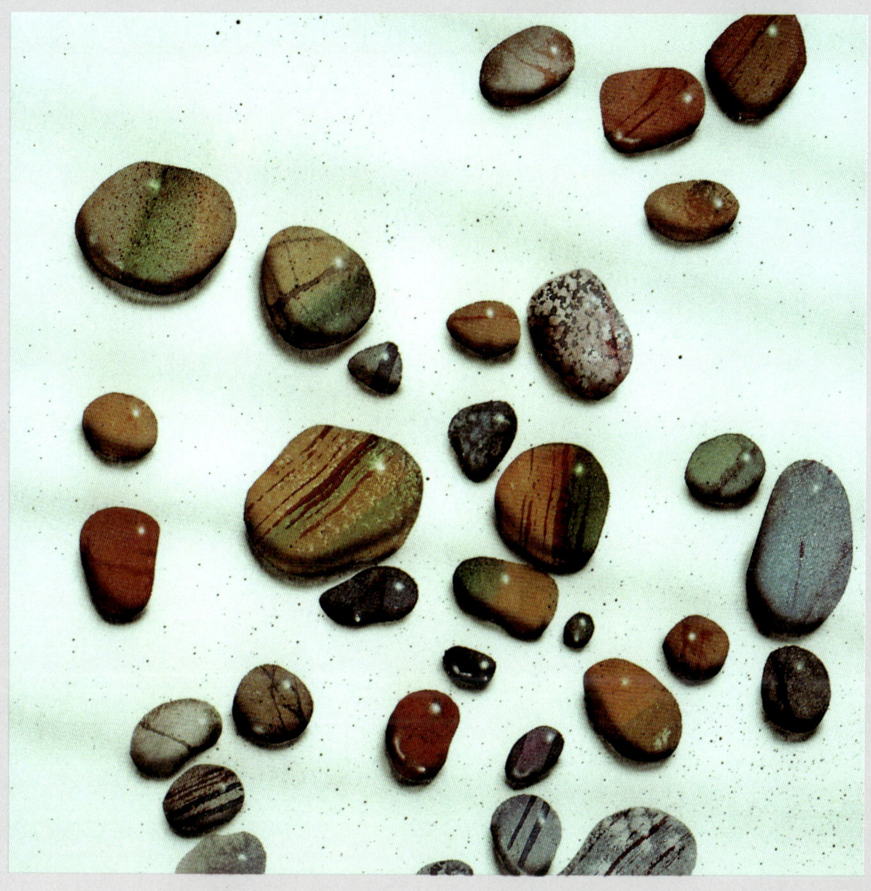

Top left

Title: *Rock Study #6*

Year: 1994

Medium: Watercolor

Size: 8" x 8"

Title: *Rock Study #8*

Year: 1994

Medium: Watercolor

Size: 8" x 8"

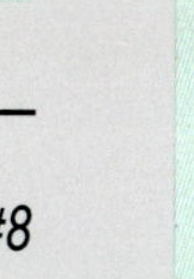

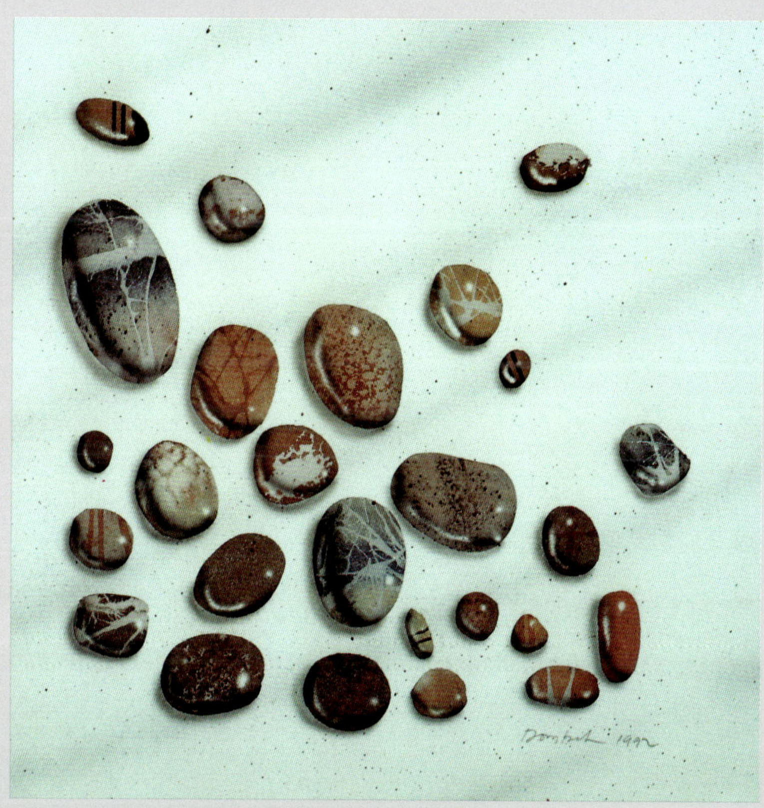

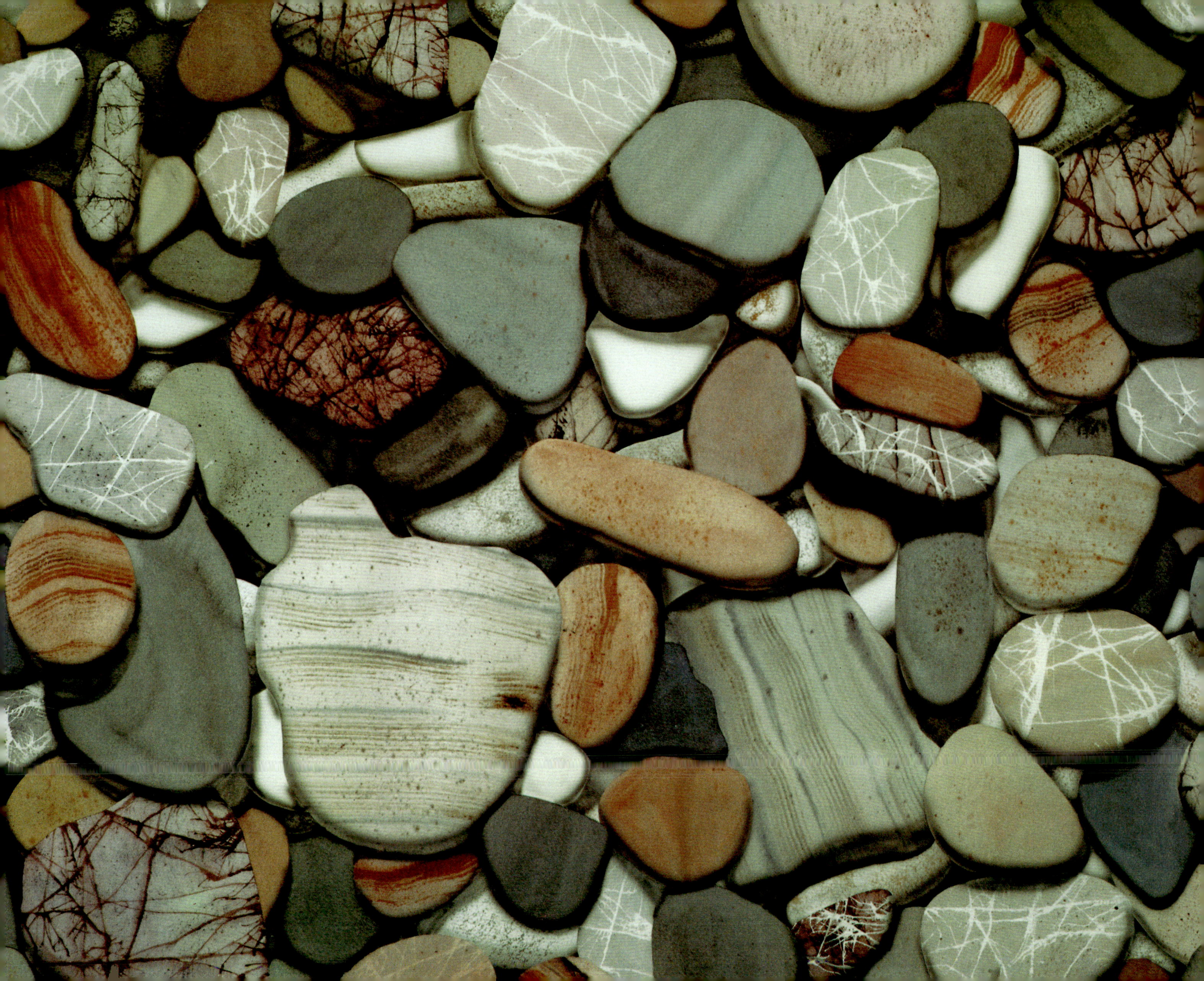

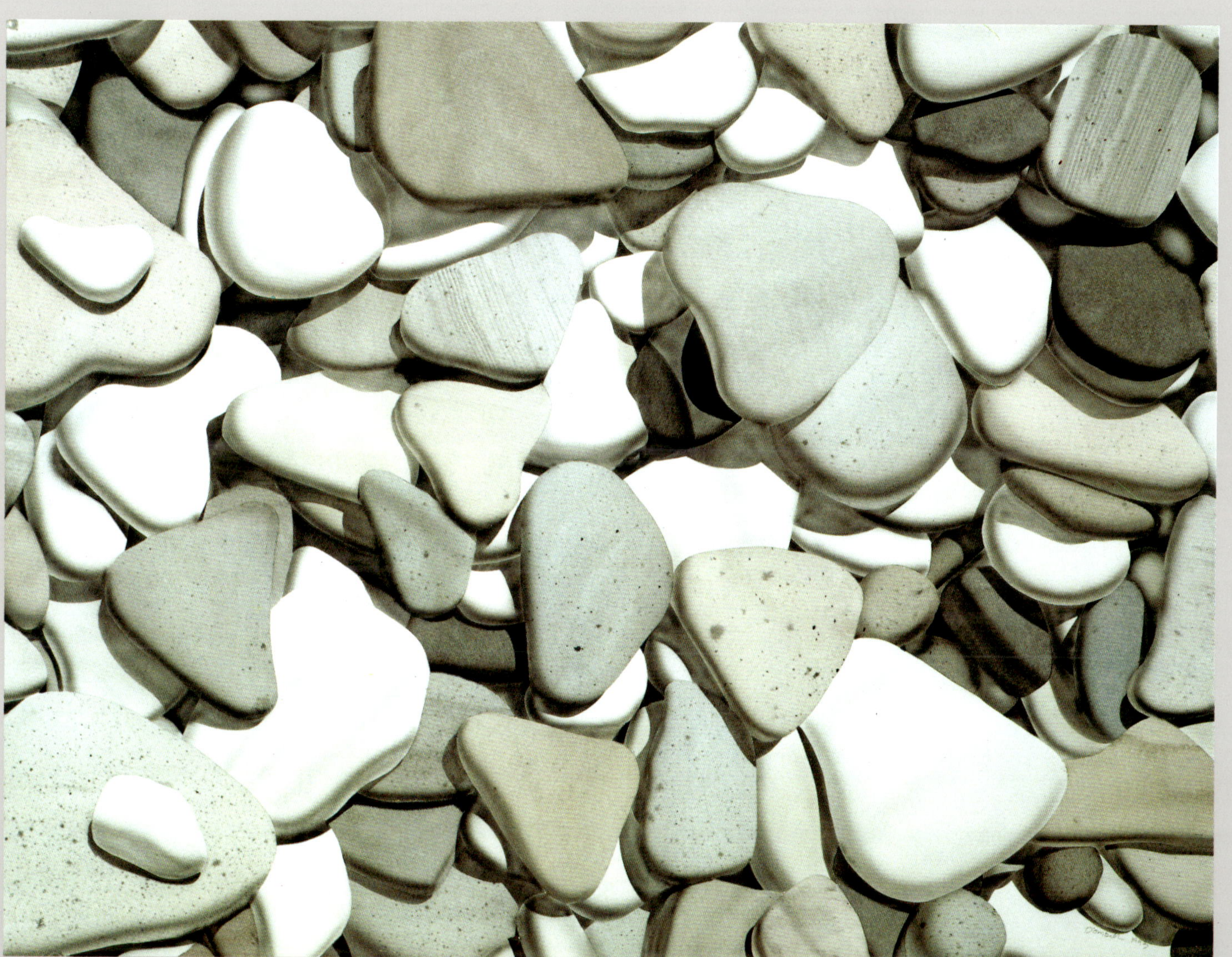

Opposite page

Title: *Red Rocks*

Year: 1994

Medium: Watercolor

Size: 30" X 42"

Title: *Washington Island*

Year: 1993

Medium: Watercolor

Size: 22" X 30"

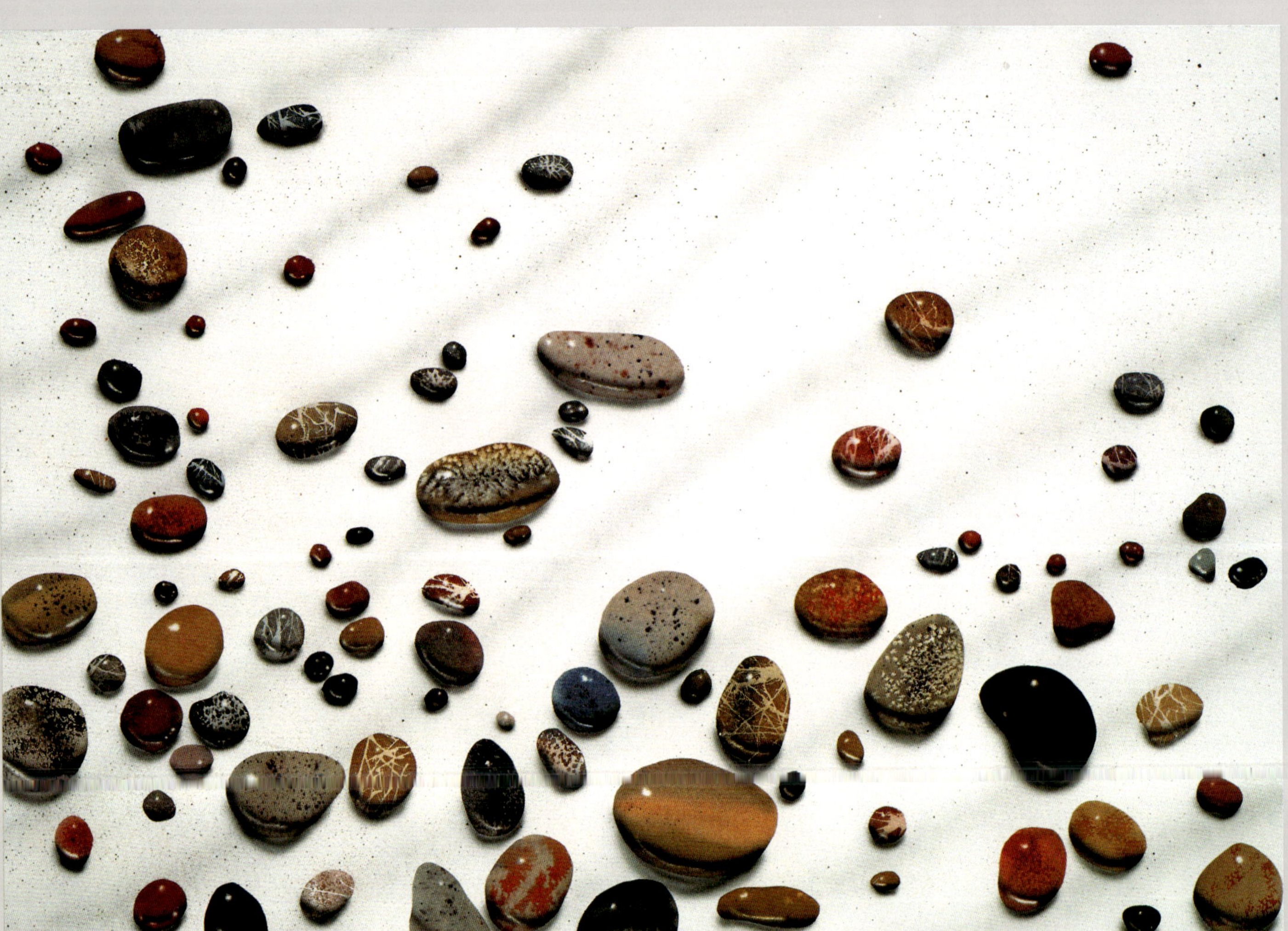

Title: *The Placement of Rocks*

Year: 1993

Medium: Watercolor

Size: 22" X 30"

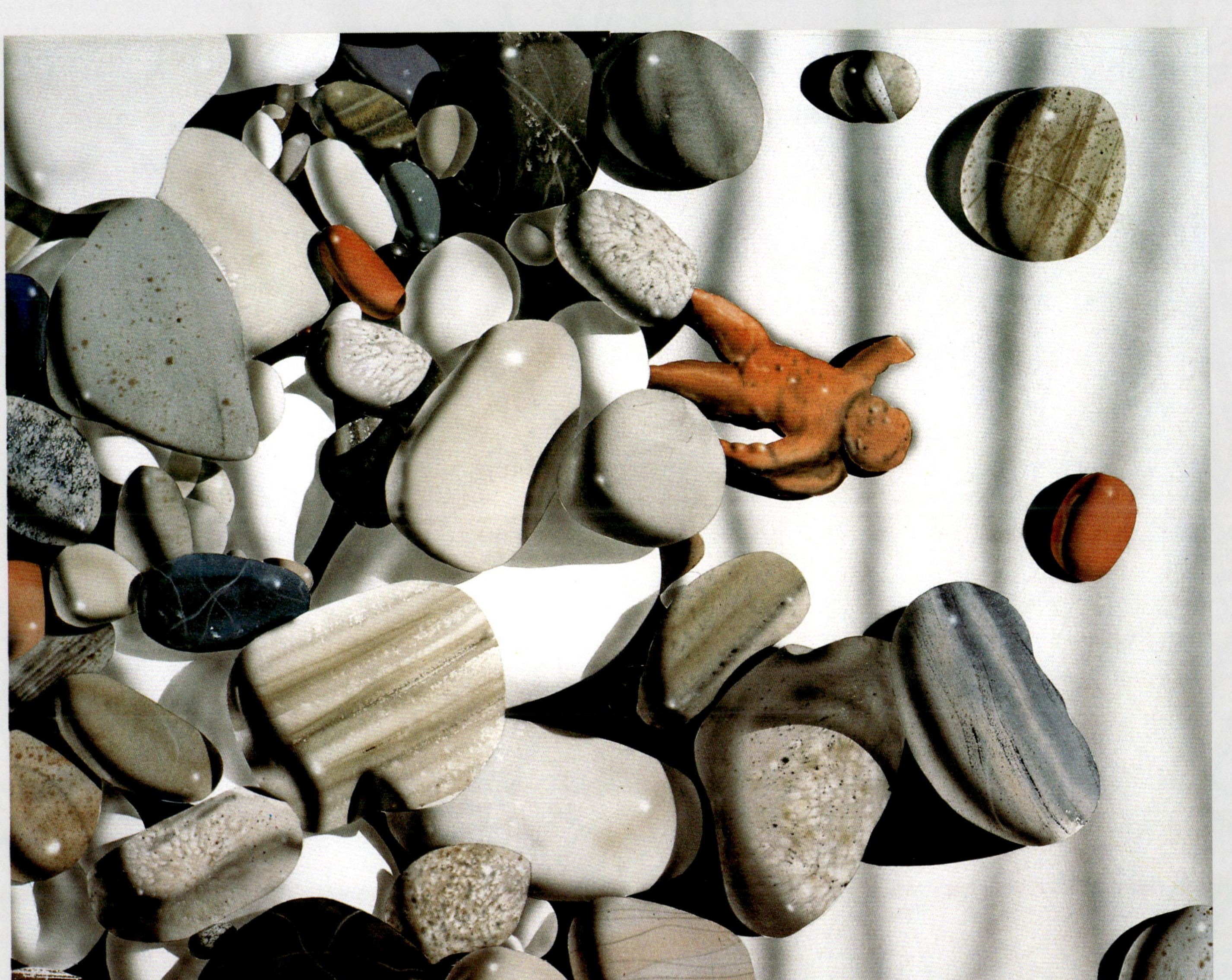

Title: *Figure in the Rocks*

Year: 1990

Medium: Watercolor

Size: 22" X 30"

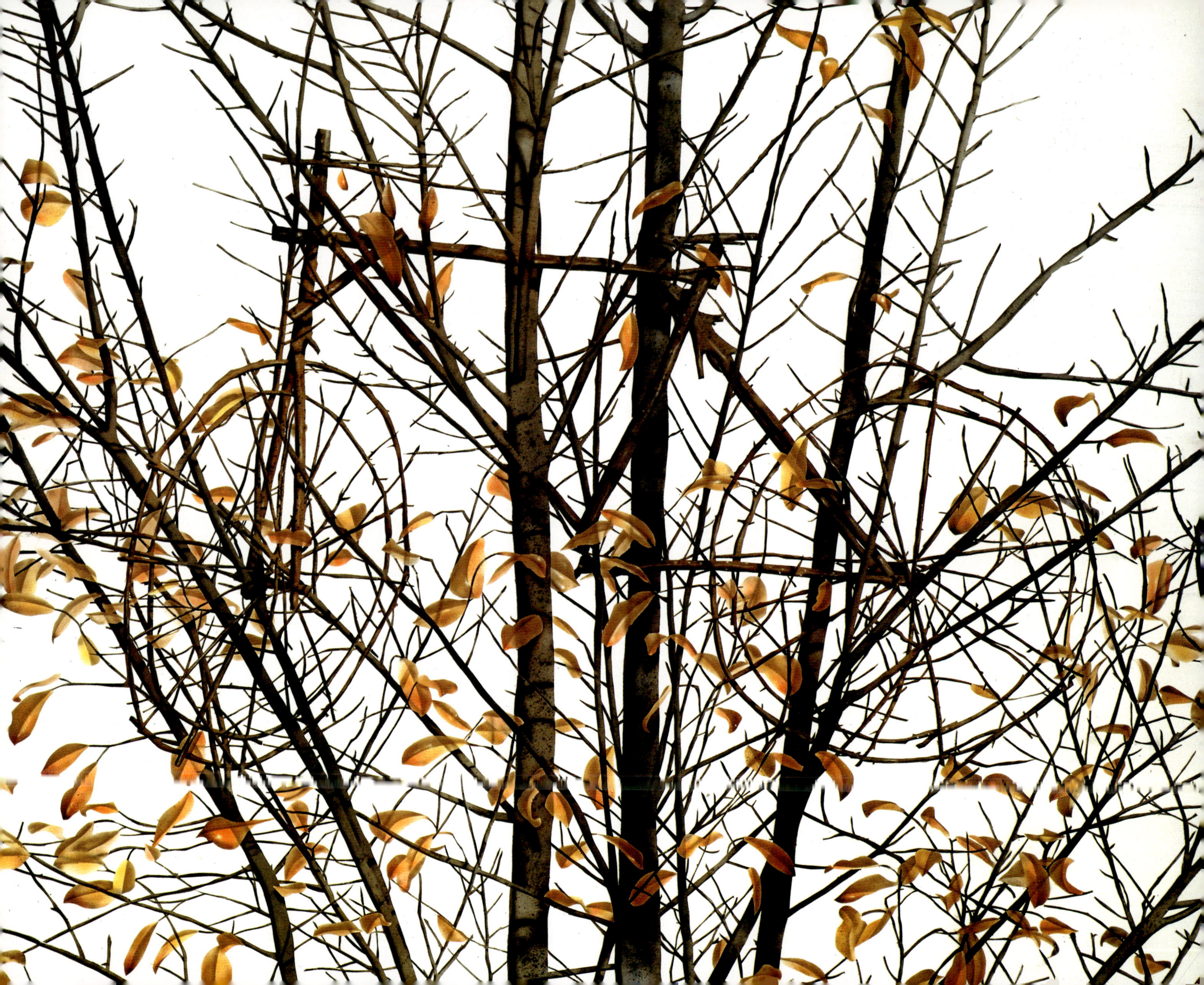

Series Six

Trees & Bikes, Bikes in Trees

1988 - 1994

When George was in Italy, he also discovered the bicycle. The subject — metallic bicycles leaning against blank walls in a harsh sunlight that leaves the heavy looming shadow of the bicycle more important than the machine itself — offered Dombek a complex counterpoint to the rock pictures, which, however, dominated his energies almost to the exclusion of the bicycles. Although the total corpus of bike pictures is relatively small compared with those he has devoted to other series, the bicycle pictures play an important link in the chain of his career, looking back in one direction to one of his student pictures, *Wheels*, of 1976, when he was first discovering the complexity of machine parts, and, more importantly, looking ahead to the "stick bike" pictures which have become an important concern of the present.

It is difficult to imagine two subjects less similar to each other than the bikes and the rocks...which may be the reason Dombek felt compelled to incorporate into the bike pictures a few of the Elba rocks, as if to say there is a relationship, the same artist did both. There is even, as one example illustrated here strongly

Opposite page

Title: *Tour de Tree*

Year: 1994

Medium: Watercolor

Size: 40" X 60"

suggests, a definite connection between the two. Most of the bike pictures have as their background simply a blank wall, or in some cases a blank wall with faint discernible architectural character, a screen upon which the sun may project the fancy shadow of the bicycle. In this one case Dombek has "taped" to that wall the trompe l'oeil representation of one of his characteristic Elba rock pictures, not just as a reminder that he was doing the rock pictures at the same time he was being "diverted" into the bicycle pictures, but also as a kind of self-referential commentary about the entire direction of his work in the making of illusionistic images. All Dombek pictures are truly trompe l'oeil. This is a painting about the making of paintings. Thus it is, in keeping with the times in art, a post modernist work.

Title: *Park in Florence*

Year: 1989

Medium: Watercolor

Size: 22" X 30"

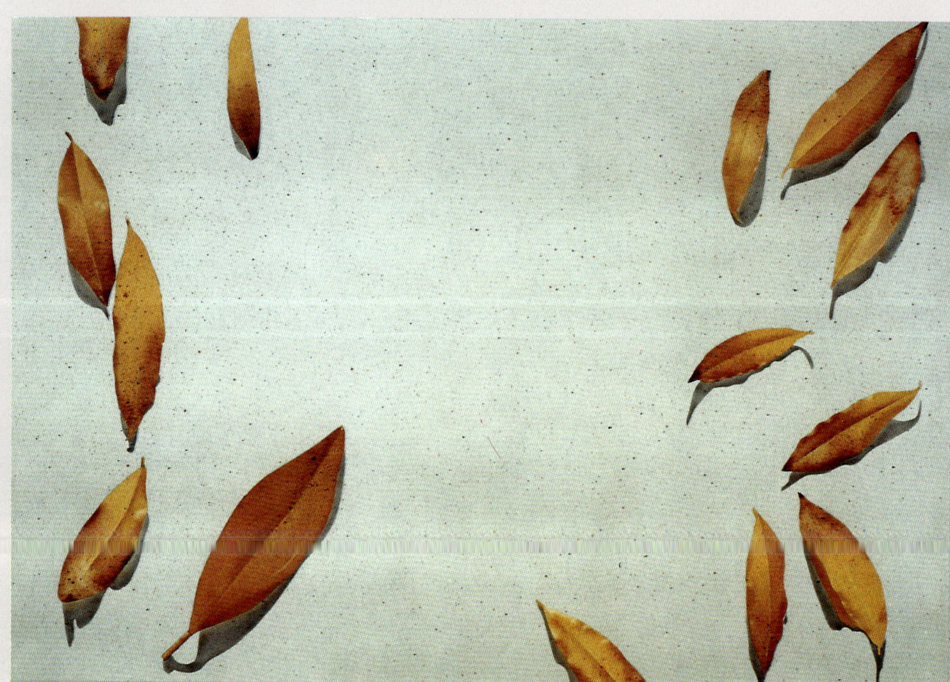

In its way it prepares us for the most stunning new departure in Dombek's career, the unquestionably post modernist series just beginning, the Stick-Bike-in-Tree series.

Even before he had commenced the curvilinear rock pictures in 1988, Dombek had done some relatively free-form botanical pictures, wild cherry trees and such, or, as in *Havana Barn* (1987) he had permitted the severe grid of the tobacco barn's timbers to be "violated" by encroaching green vines climbing along them.

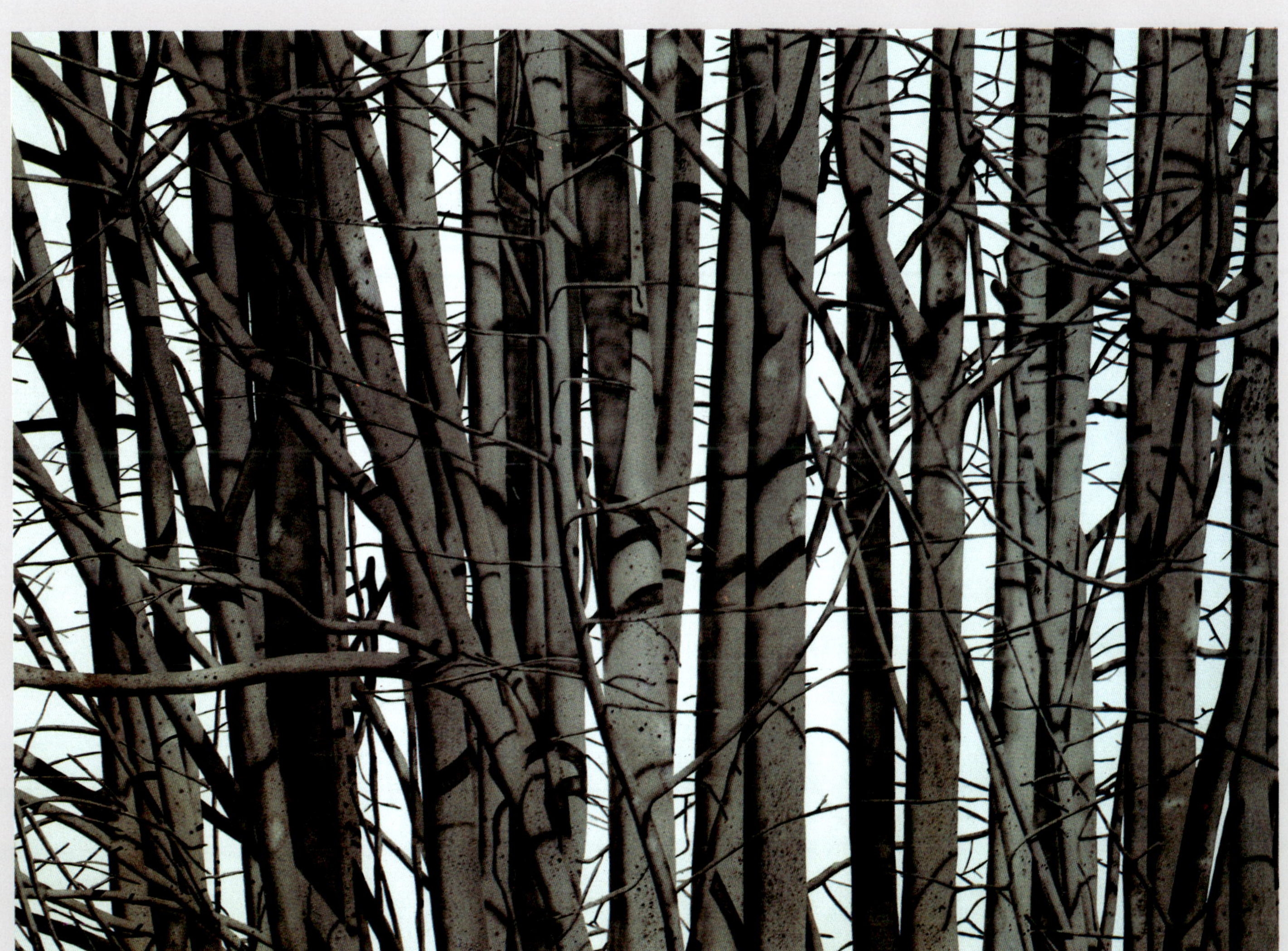

Title: *Tree Grid*

Year: 1991

Medium: Watercolor

Size: 30" X 42"

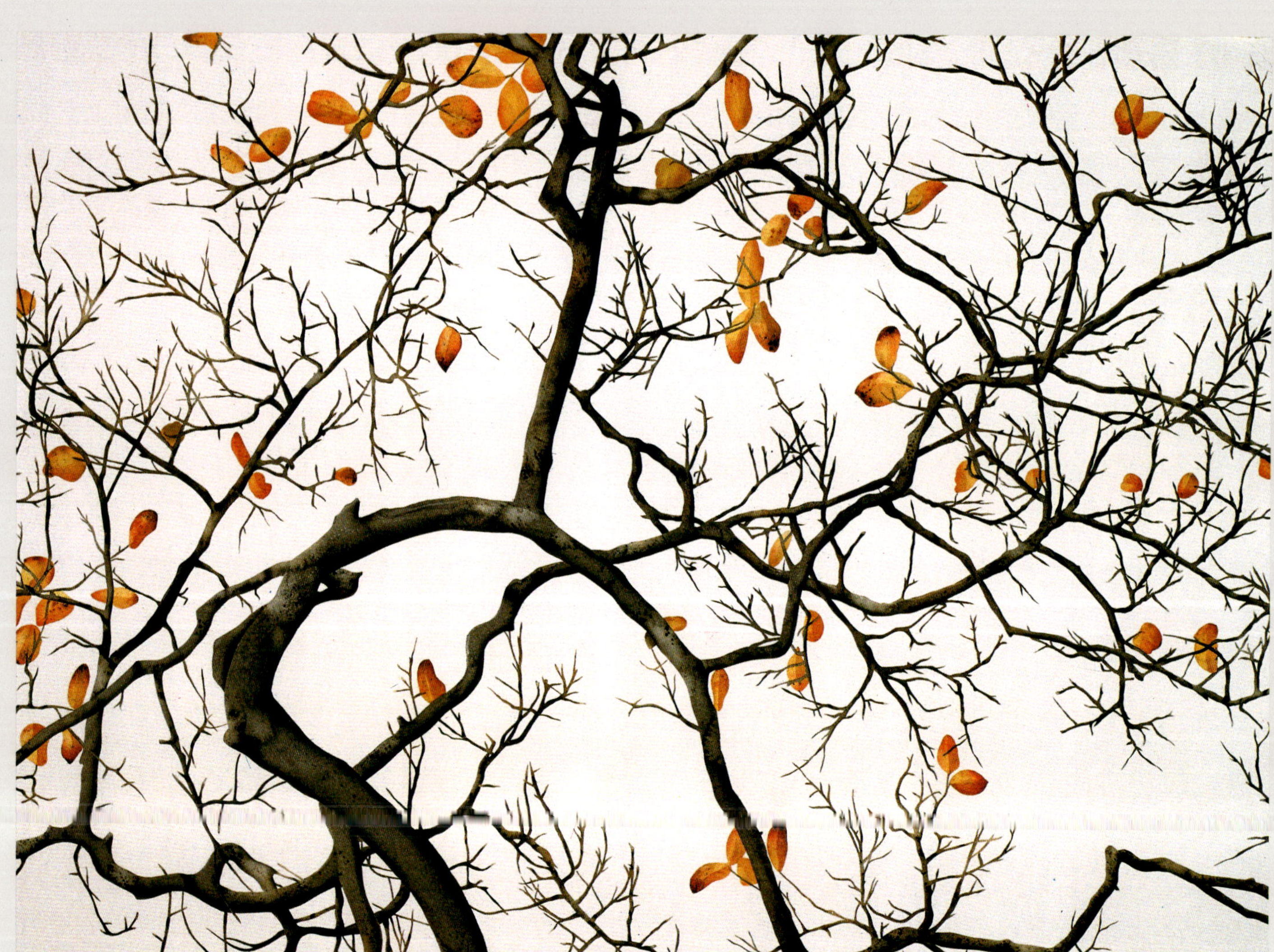

Title: *Tree of Life*

Year: 1988

Medium: Watercolor

Size: 40" X 60"

Dombek's pictures of trees —svelte graceful trunks with a few random leaves dangling from prickly boughs — are his most quiet, most still, most serene paintings. At the same time, because of the total lack of any geometric structure and because they are taken directly from nature, they are his most romantic art.

Here then was the artist setting off his exemplary geometric art with a concurrent organic tendency. Painting rocks and trees with his left hand while painting bicycles with his right (metaphorically speaking, since he is not ambidextrous), Dombek suddenly conceived of the idea of combining the bike and the tree: not literally propping a metallic bicycle against a cherry tree but constructing out of wild cherry boughs a bicycle and propping the "invention" into a cherry tree. For at least the last ten years, Dombek has had a personal habit, perhaps superstitious, of...but let him tell it.

"Everywhere I moved to I have gathered a couple dozen sticks and haphazardly constructed a very literal abstract relief piece to hang on the wall. Now that I think about it, it seems my way of

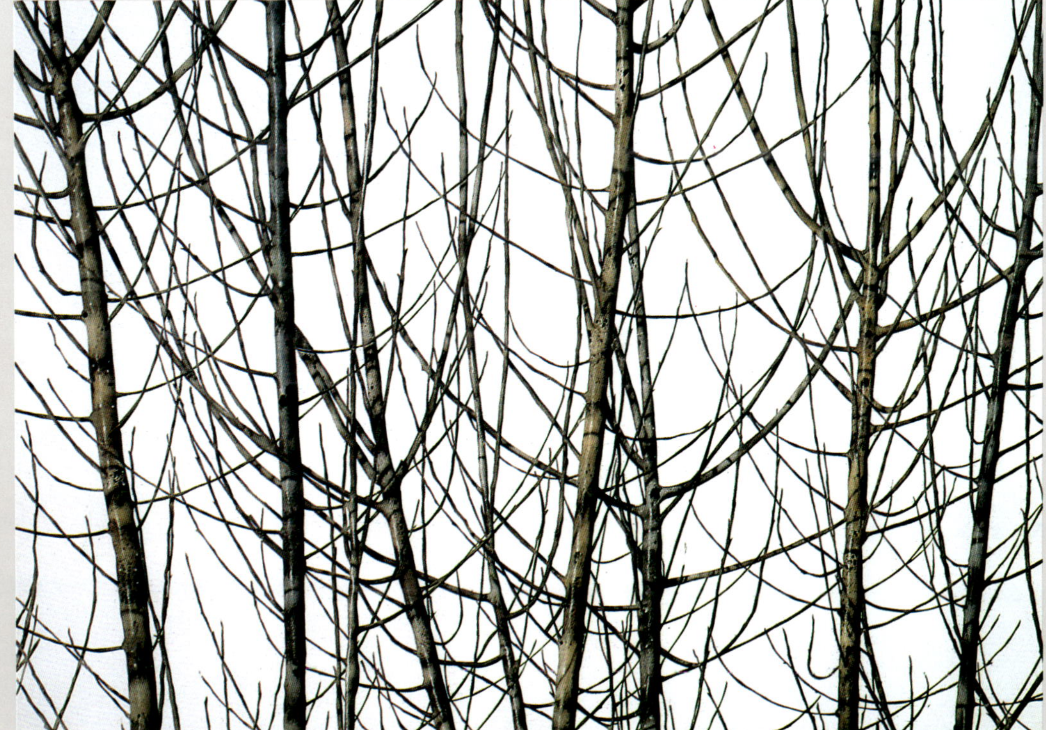

Title: *Tree Line*

Year: 1991

Medium: Watercolor

Size: 30" X 42"

claiming the space. With each move, and I've moved often, I simply took the piece down and discarded it and built a new piece at the new home."[21]

When he moved into his large Tallahassee studio in an industrial park, the first thing he did was create an abstract construction of sticks and hang it on his wall. Staring at it one day while metaphorically working with his left hand on a picture of trees and his right hand on a picture of bicycles, he suddenly saw a connection between the spokes of a bicycle and the limbs of the tree, and he was inspired to fashion some sticks into a bicycle. The next step naturally was to replace the metallic bicycle, gleaming in the sunlight against its blank wall, with the stick bicycle, but the stick bicycle couldn't take the place of the real metal bike; it didn't belong there. So he propped it into a tree.

Or, rather, in his imagination he superimposed the bike on a tree, and, further, in his imagination he made the bicycle blue and made some of the tree leaves blue as well. This liberation of his fantasy, which for so many years had been subdued by the appearances of things, catapulted him into a new direction, but left him very unsettled by it.

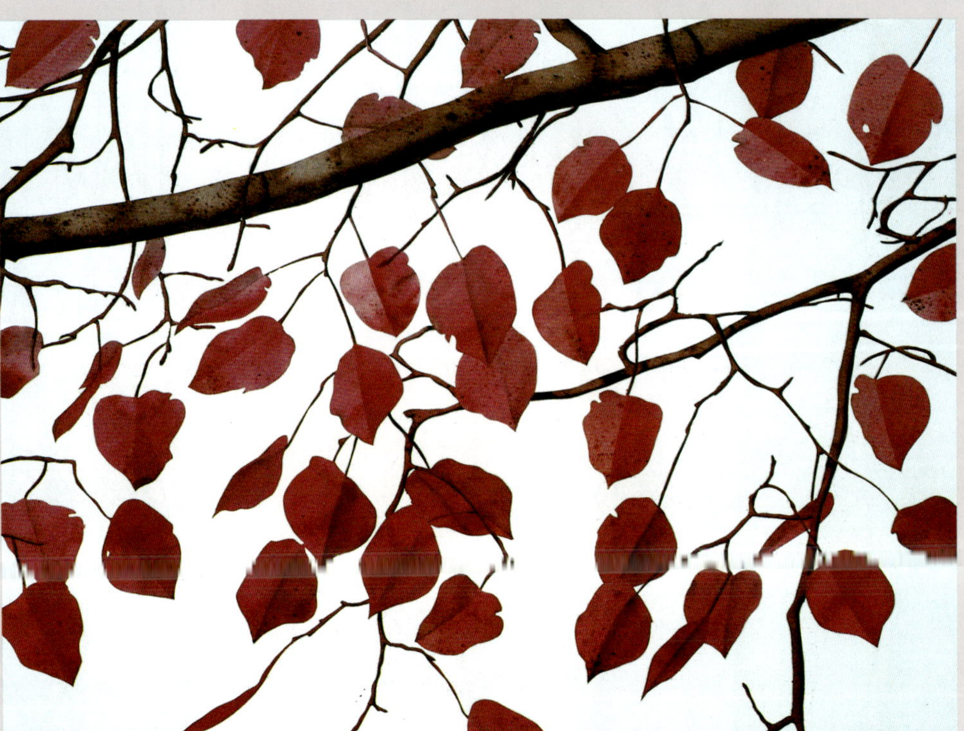

Title: *Red Heart Leaves*

Year: 1994

Medium: Watercolor

Size: 22" X 30"

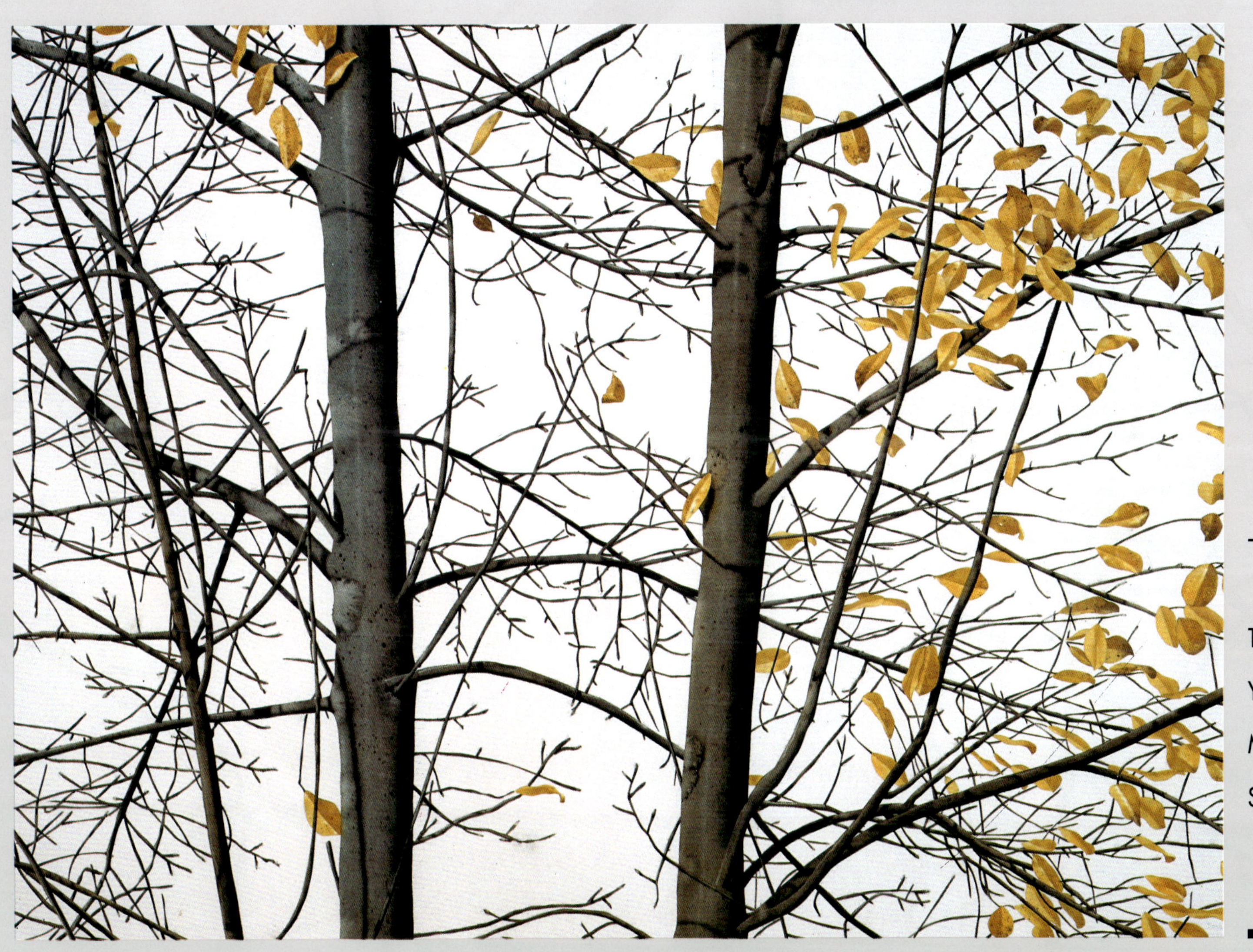

Title: *Dialog*

Year: 1988

Medium: Watercolor

Size: 40" X 60"

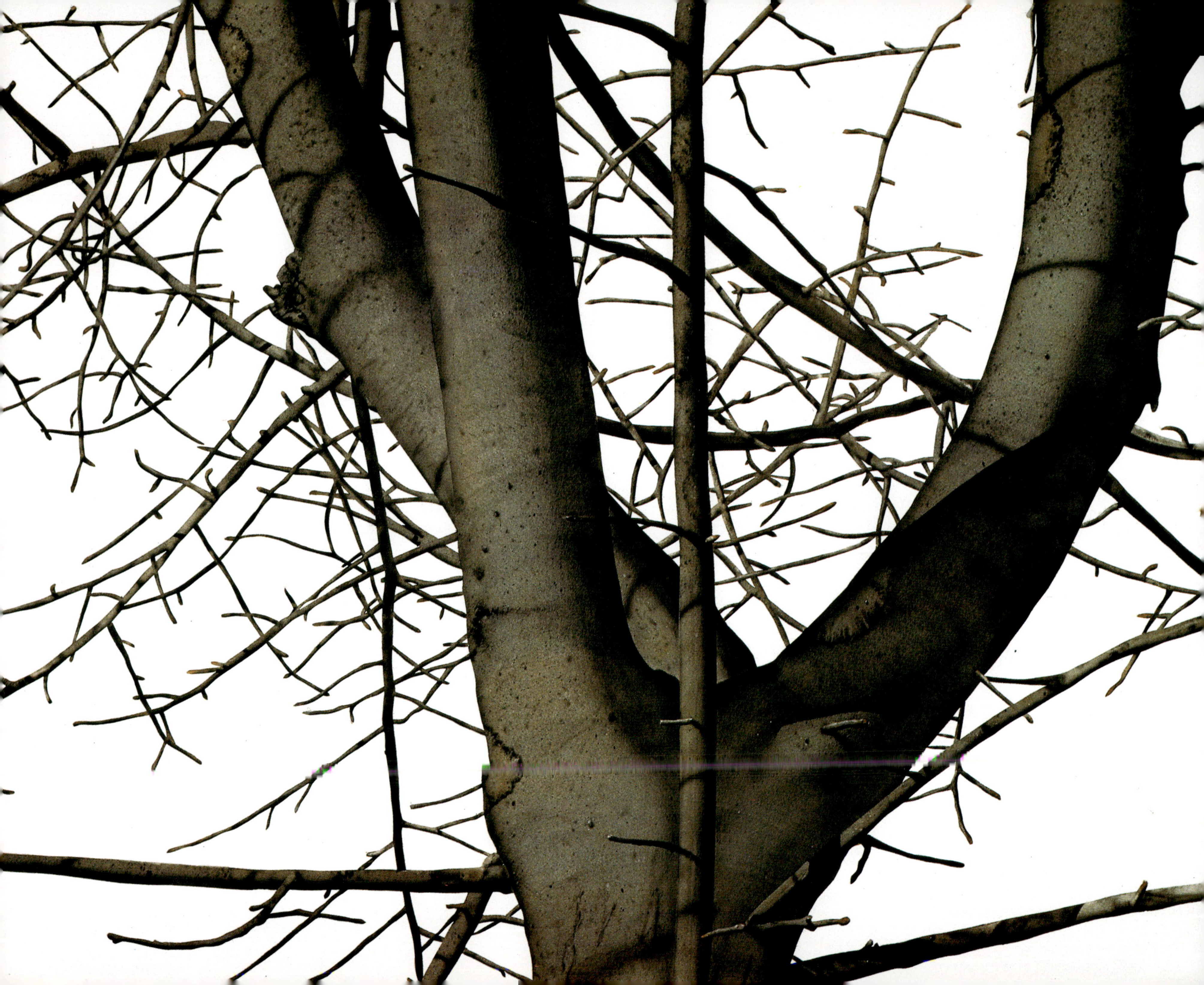

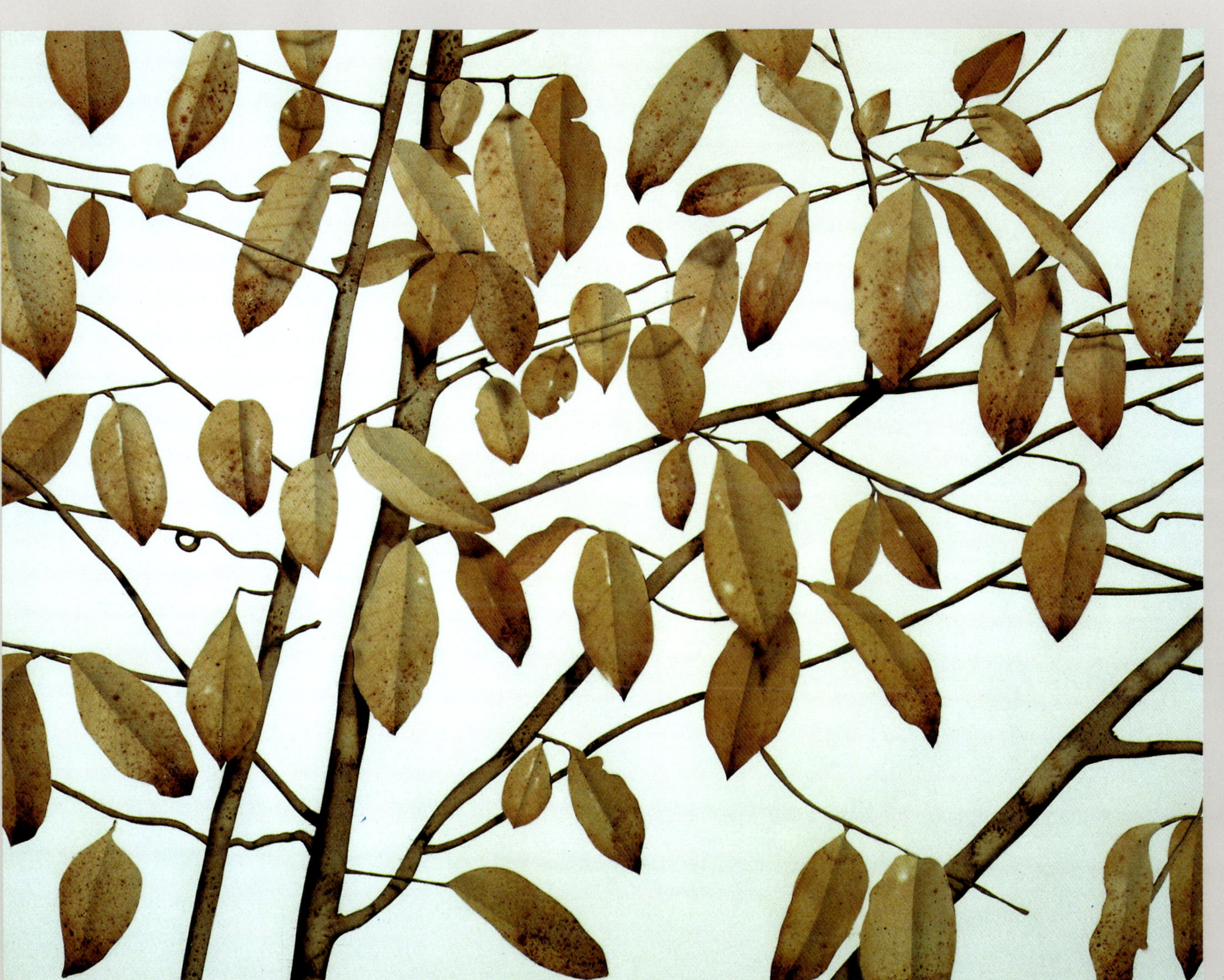

Opposite page

Title: *Birch Tree*

Year: 1990

Medium: Watercolor

Size: 40" X 60"

Title: *Golden Leaves*

Year: 1994

Medium: Watercolor

Size: 22" X 30"

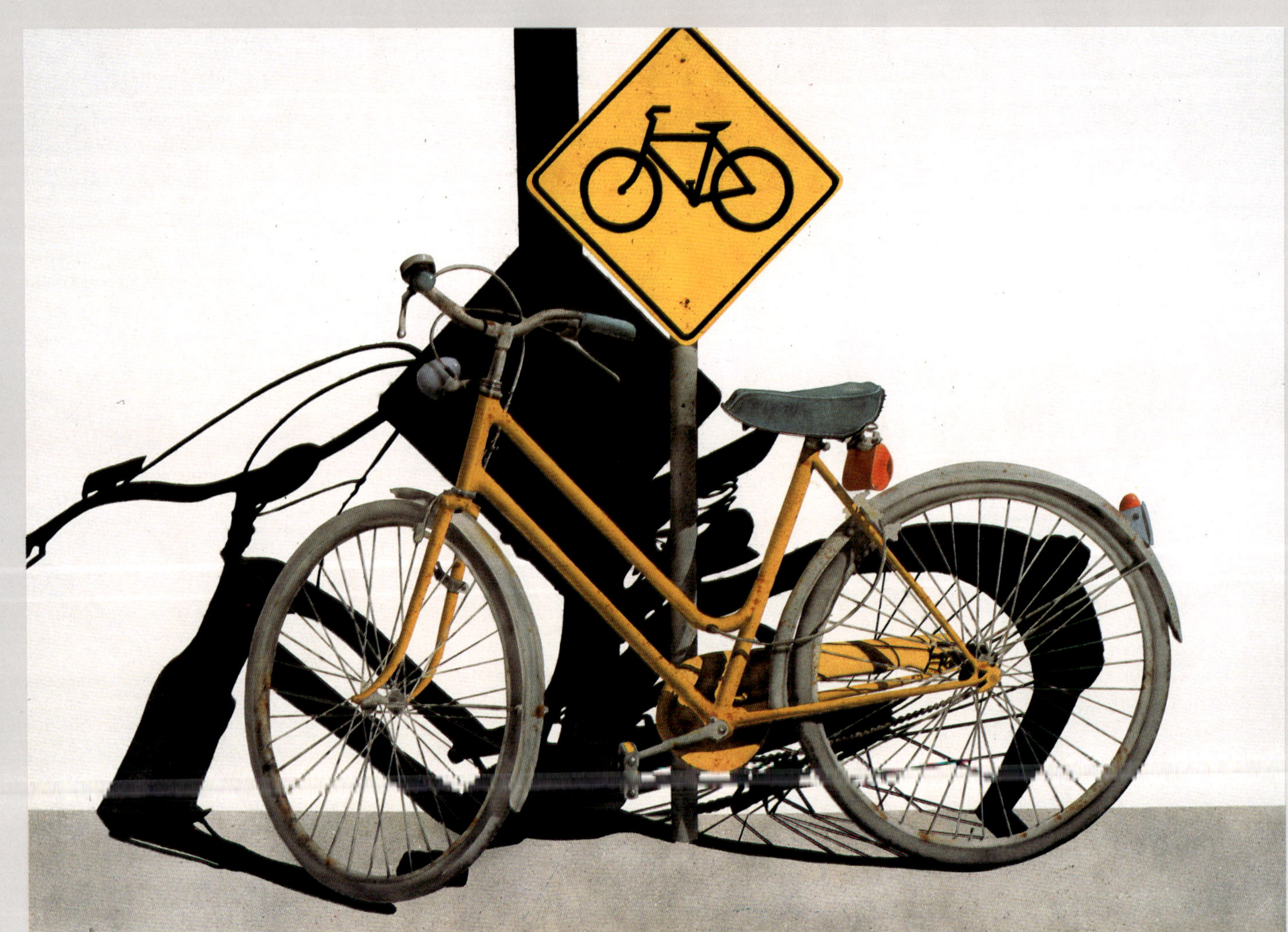

Title: *The Streets of Florence*

Year: 1991

Medium: Watercolor

Size: 40" X 60"

"I have been disturbed at all crossroads that have brought about changes in the development of my work,"[22] he has said.

Dombek is reluctant to talk about this crossroads. He has completed only a dozen bike-in-tree pictures and feels that it may be premature to get excited over the new direction. He does not know where the work will lead him; he has not outlined the "climax" or even the individual chapters of his work's novel; the excitement of creation, for him, is in the discovery.

Dombek paints a picture — or rather a whole series of 200 variations on a theme — to find out why he has painted it. No two of his series are sufficiently alike that he might be accused of having a fixed subject matter. He was born in Arkansas, grew up in it and was nurtured in its wild places, then spent years "in exile" outside of the state, but eventually came back to it. Arkansas is in his blood, and it has shaped him, and he has shaped his

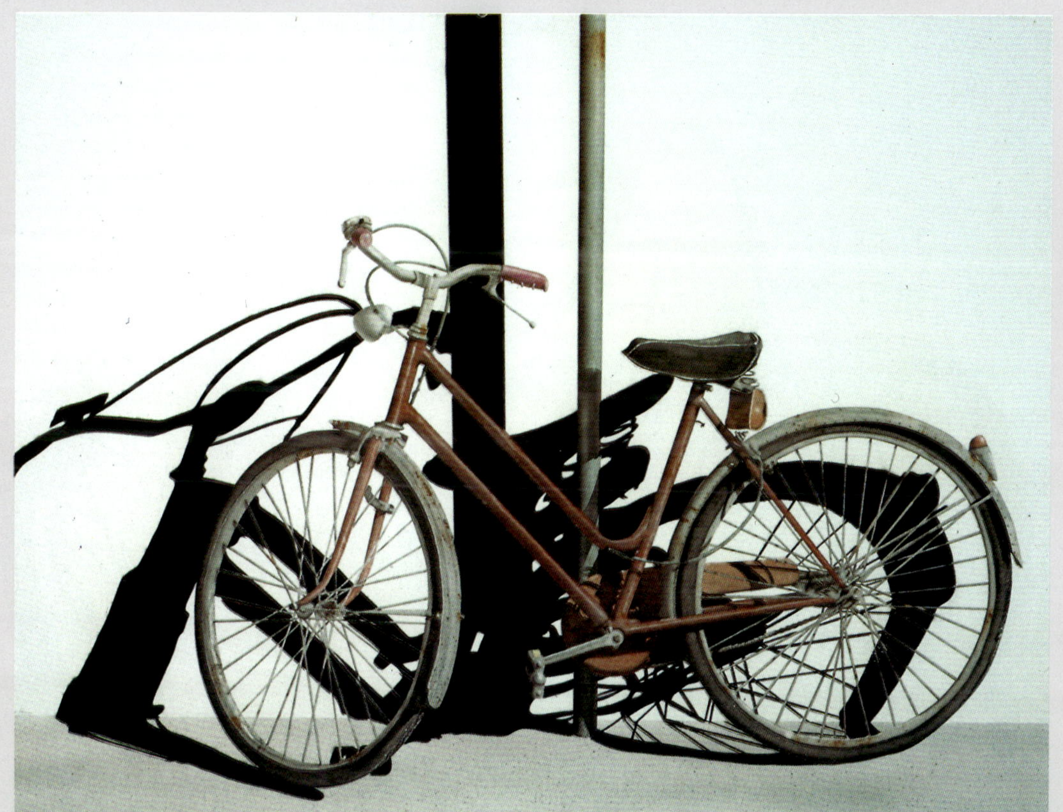

Title: *Karen's Bike*

Year: 1993

Medium: Watercolor

Size: 30" X 42"

art in a cherishing of her.

This retrospective exhibition, and this book accompanying it, ought to make the paintings of George Dombek available to a large public, and make it possible to view the several series of Dombek's work in the continuity of their creation. He is one of the most highly respected and well known artists to come out of Arkansas, and he has produced a large, impressive body of work which will endure and leave a permanent impression upon the history of art. ■

Title: *Palazzo Medici*

Year: 1991

Medium: Watercolor

Size: 40" X 60"

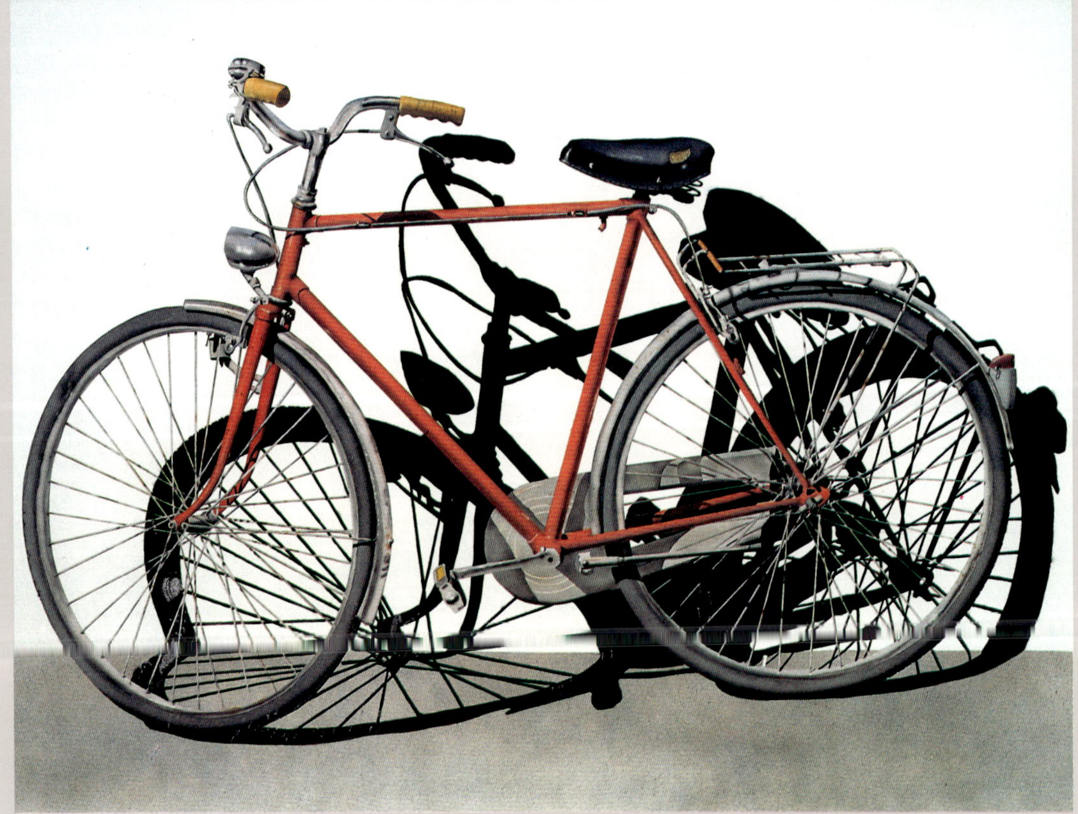

Donald Harington is Professor of Art History at the University of Arkansas in Fayetteville. He has an MFA in printmaking from the University of Arkansas, an MA in art history from Boston University and worked on a doctorate in art history at Harvard. Some of his best work includes **Let Us Build Us A City** (a Purter Prize winner), **The Architecture of the Arkansas Ozarks** and **Some Other Place: The Right Place** which was made into the movie, **"Return."**

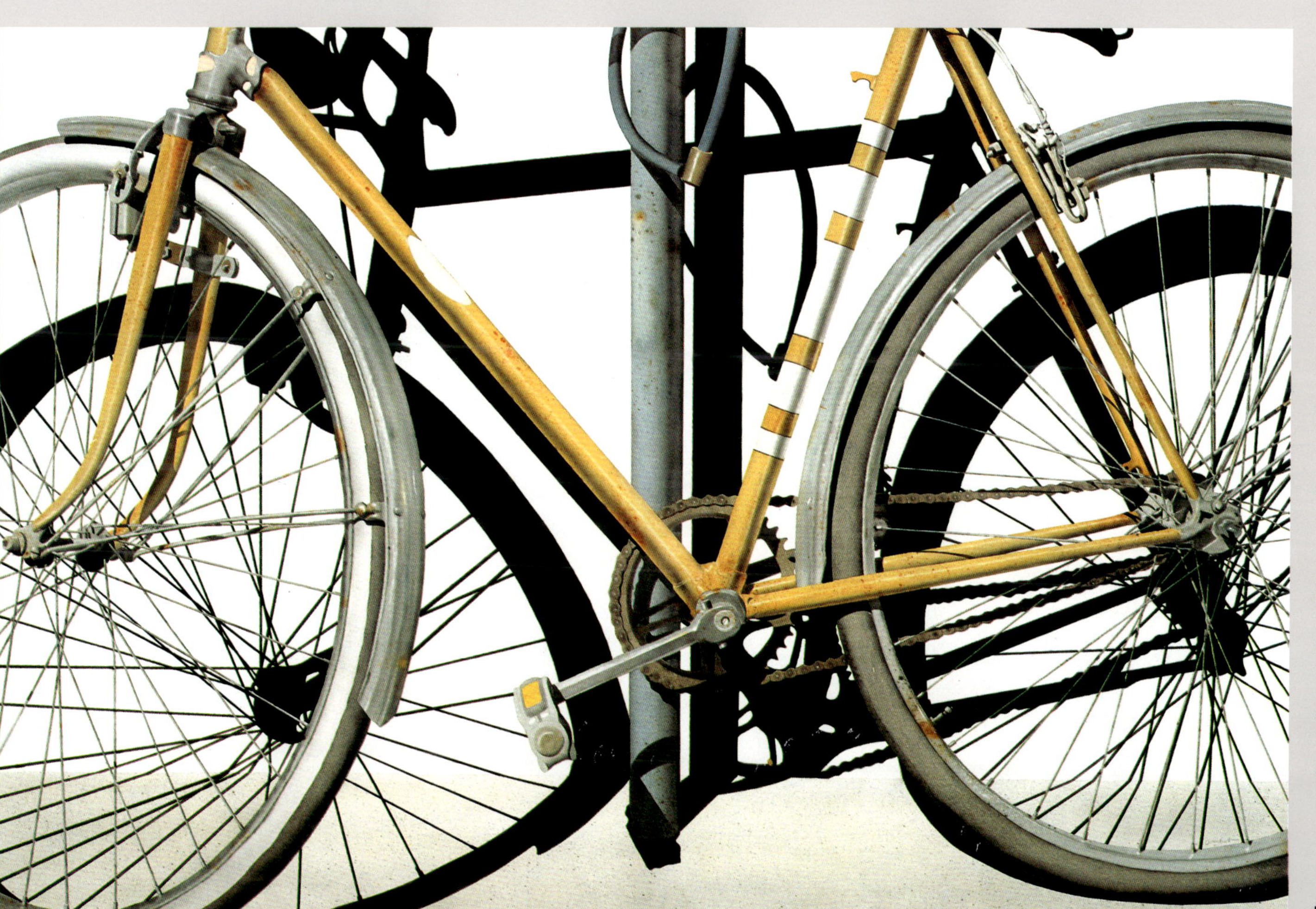

Title: *Yellow Bicycle*

Year: 1991

Medium: Watercolor

Size: 40" X 60"

Opposite page

Title: *Stick Bike*

Year: 1994

Medium: Watercolor

Size: 30" X 42"

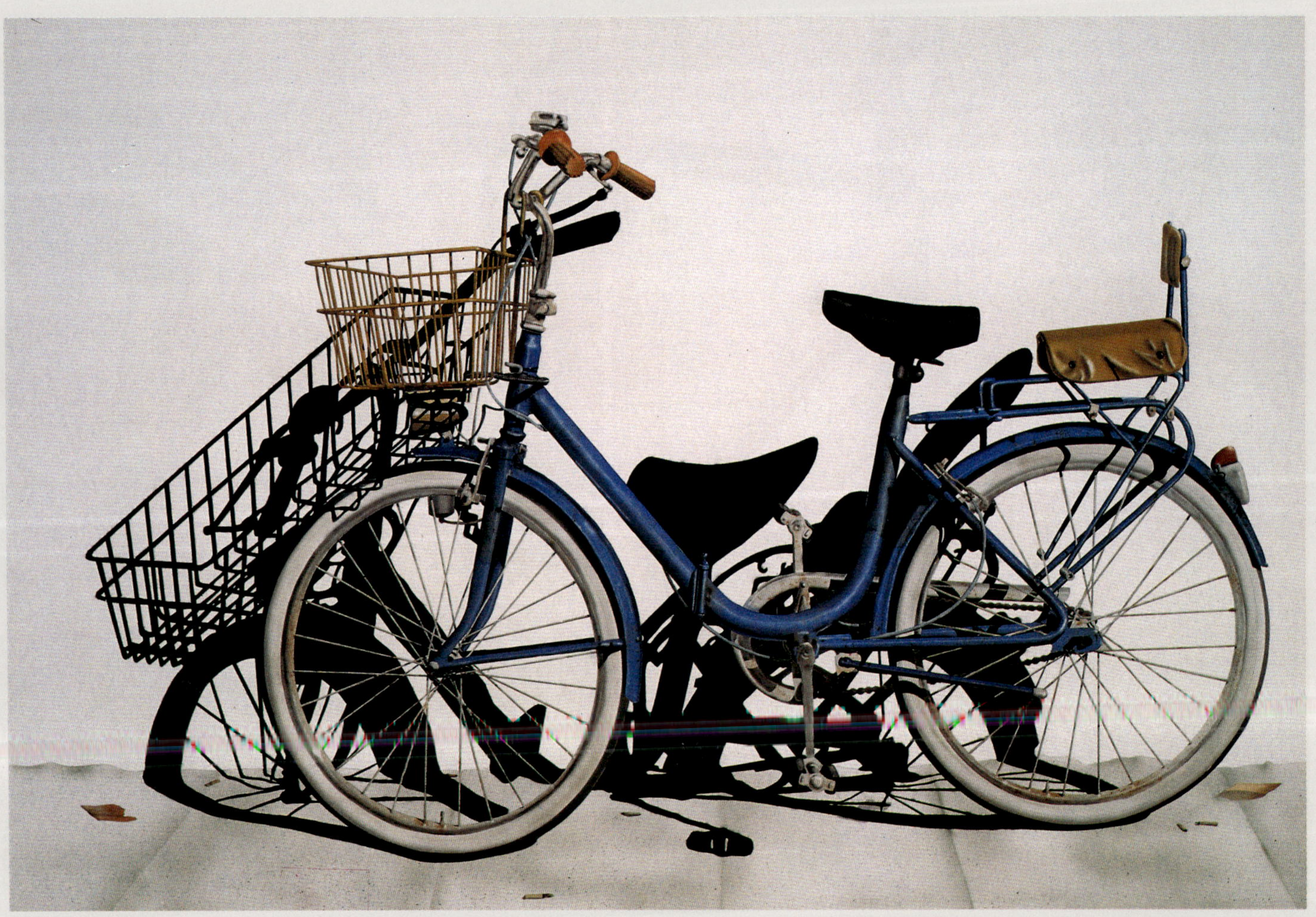

Title: *Yellow Seat*

Year: 1991

Medium: Watercolor

Size: 40" X 60"

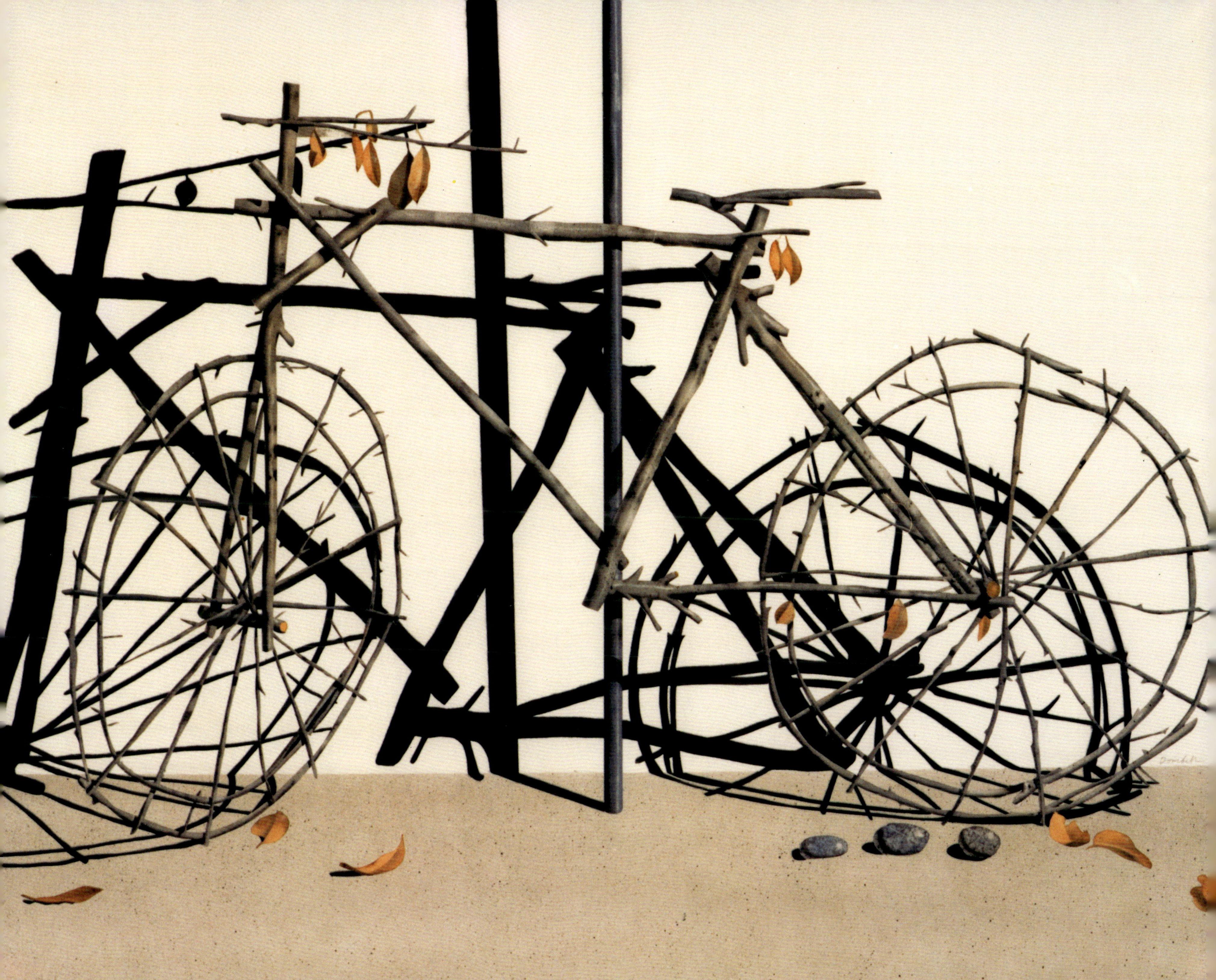

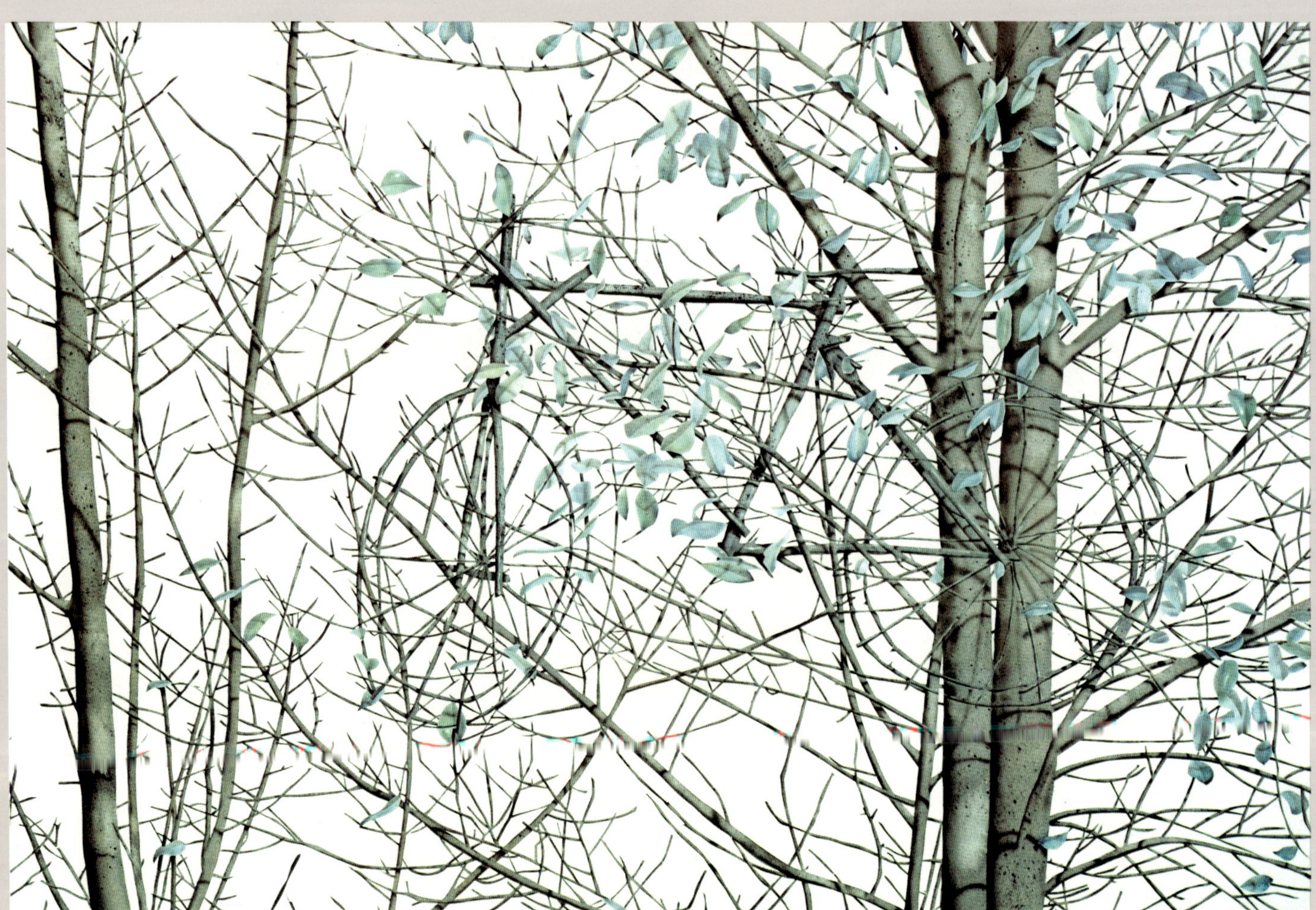

Title: *Top Flight*

Year: 1994

Medium: Watercolor

Size: 30" X 1[illegible]"

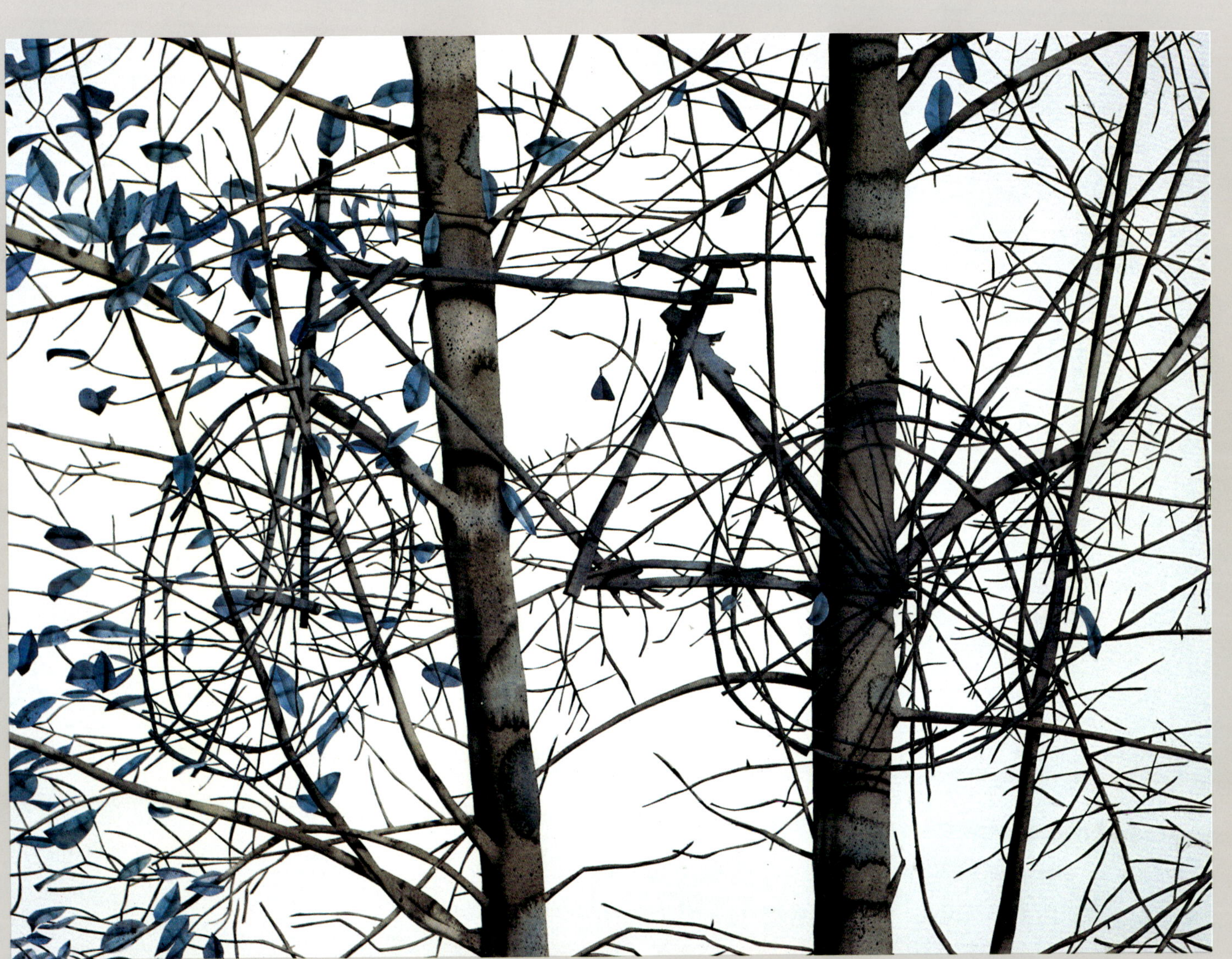

Title: *Touring*

Year: 1994

Medium: Watercolor

Size: 30" X 42"

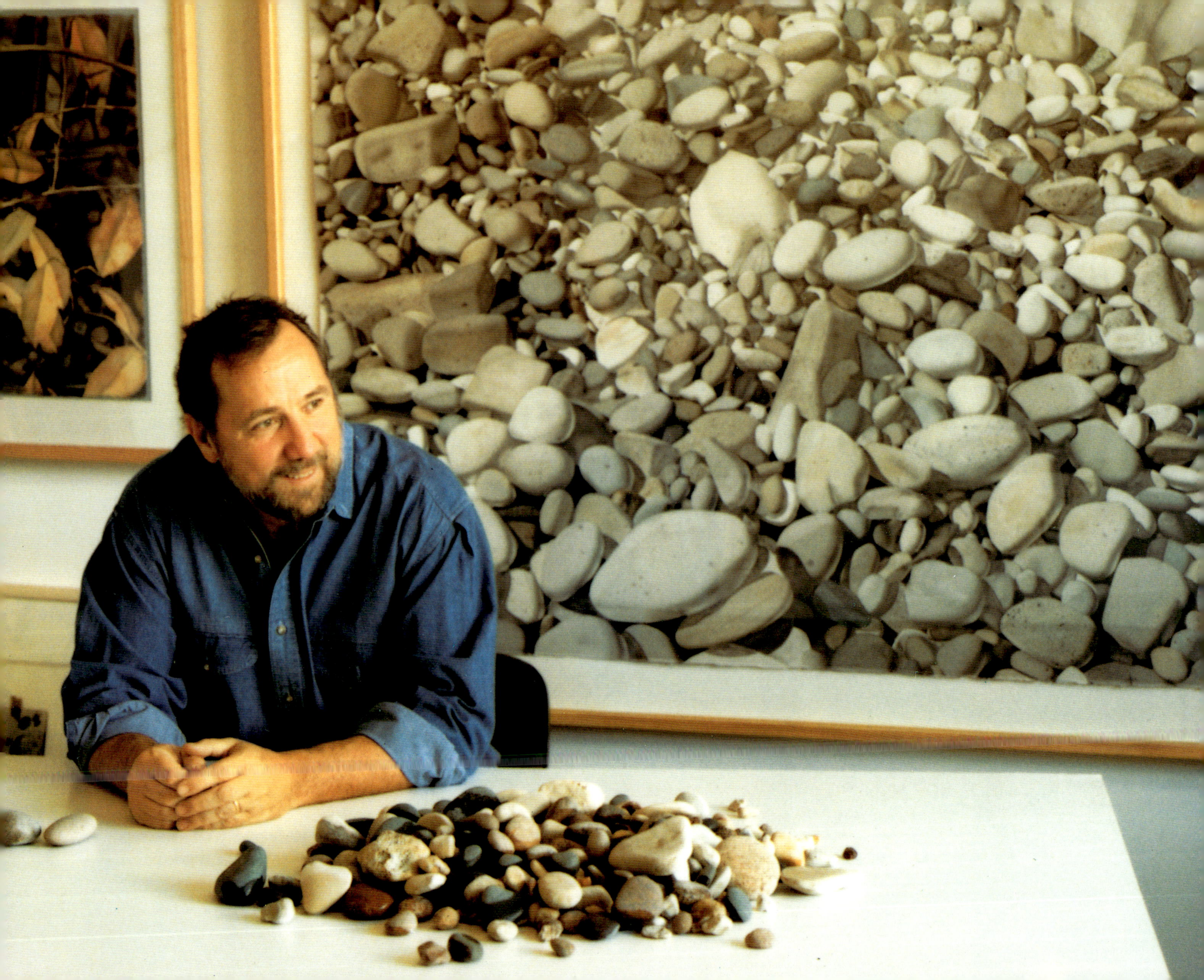

A Biographical Sketch

George Dombek

Born in Arkansas, George Dombek received his Bachelor of Architecture and Master's of Fine Arts in Painting from the University of Arkansas. Since then he has taught at several universities, including Youngstown State University, the University of Arkansas, Florida A&M University, King Faisal University in Saudi Arabia and Florida State University in Florence, Italy.

He has been the recipient of more than 80 awards, including the Southern Arts Federation, the National Endowment of the Arts Regional Visual Arts Fellowship (1994), the Florida Artist Fellowship (1993, 1985), and has paintings in more than 600 private, corporate and museum collections, including the Arkansas Arts Center, Birmingham Museum of Art, Butler Institute of American Art and the Carnegie Museum of Art.

Since 1977 he has exhibited in more than 30 one-man shows and more than 100 group exhibitions, including shows at the San Francisco Museum of Art and the Scottsdale Center for the Arts.

George Dombek's love affair with watercolors began more than 30 years ago, when he was a high school art student in Paris, Arkansas. His first subjects were Ozark landscapes. After graduate school, he moved to San Francisco and began 15 years of painting manmade structures and architectural elements.

In 1988, his work began to change, focusing instead on the random order found in nature, primarily trees and leaves. The years 1988 and 1989 were spent painting and teaching in Florence, Italy.

That wonderful year gave him the opportunity to explore the city streets, where he found inspiration in the shadows cast by bicycles and the light reflected in leaves on the ground. When not teaching in the city, he traveled the country's western coast, where he was mesmerized by the patterns and colors found in the rocks that covered the beaches of Cinque Terre and the Isle of Elba — fragments of the marble and porphyry that had been mined by the Romans centuries earlier.

Since returning to the United States, he has continued to paint the same subjects, interpreted now in bicycles built in his studio from wild cherry twigs. The rocks he paints now are gathered from the shores of the Great Lakes and other native locales.

"Through all the years and so many different subjects, there has been a recurring theme: the deliberate order of architecture and the random order found in nature," he says. "There has always been a single goal in my work — to capture that silent order and, in it, provide a quiet place for meditation. The best of my paintings achieve that." ■

Opposite page

In his studio, the artist:

George Dombek

P.O. Box 215

Goshen, Arkansas

72735

1(800) 7-DOMBEK

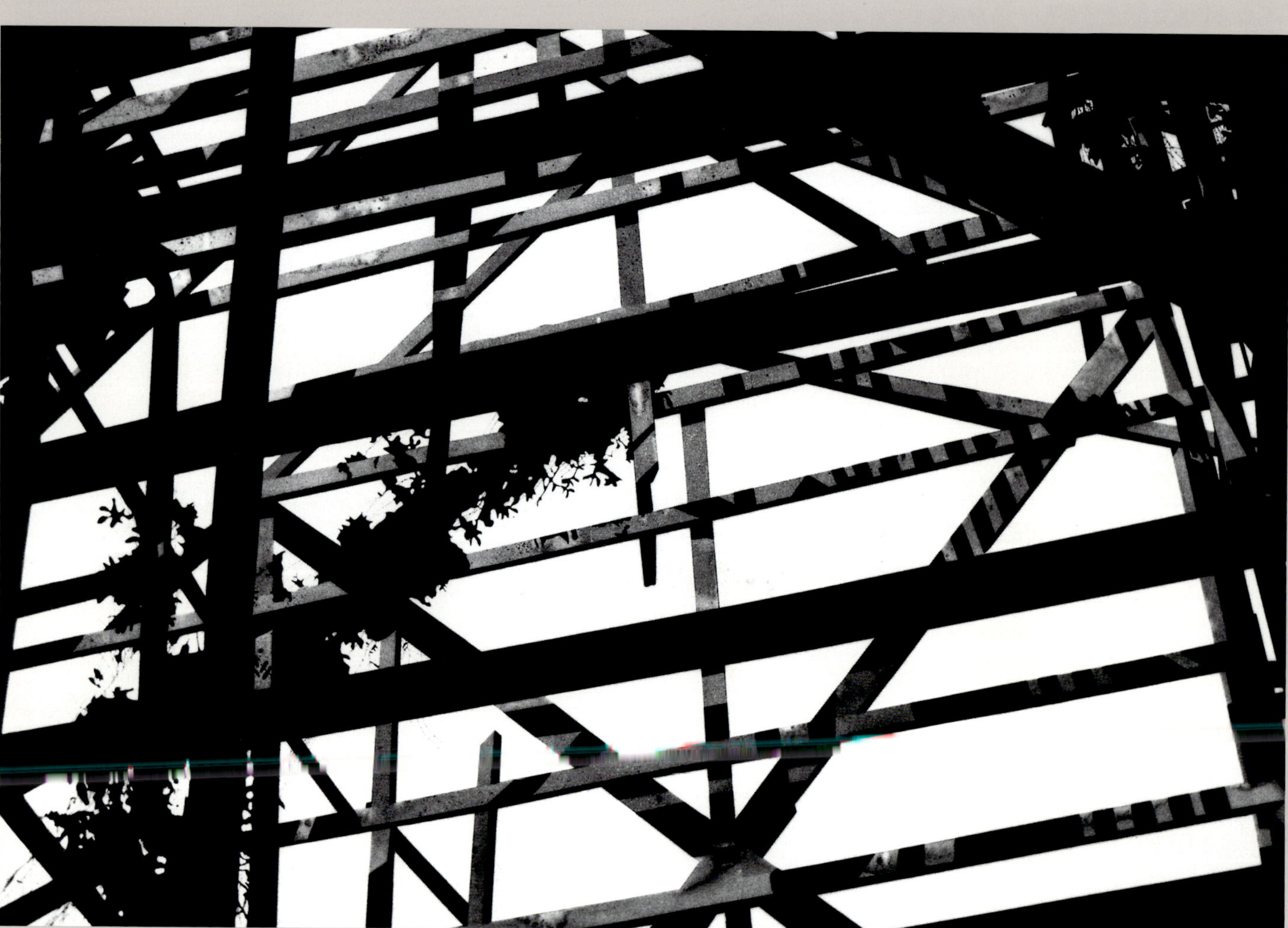

Title: *Barn 'X'*

Year: 1987

Medium: Watercolor

Size: 30" X 43"

One-Man Exhibitions

1995 University of Arkansas, Fayetteville
University of Central Arkansas, Conway

1994 Arkansas Arts Center, Little Rock, Arkansas
Chroma Gallery, Little Rock, Arkansas
Nice Picture Gallery, Havana, Florida

1993 Nan Miller Gallery, Rochester, New York

1992 Leslie Levy Fine Arts, Scottsdale, Arizona

1991 Rosenfeld Gallery, Philadelphia, Pennsylvania

1990 Florida A & M University, Tallahassee, Florida
621 Gallery, Tallahassee, Florida

1988 Butler Institute of American Art, Youngstown, Ohio
Florida A & M University, Tallahassee, Florida

1987 O.K. South Works of Art, Miami, Florida

1986 Fay Gold Gallery, Atlanta, Georgia
Lemoyne Center for Visual Arts, Tallahassee, Florida

1985 Florida Center for Contemporary Art, Tampa
Gallery Contemporanea, Jacksonville, Florida
Florida A & M University, Tallahassee, Florida

1984 The Savannah College of Art and Design, Savannah, Georgia
The University of Tampa, Tampa, Florida

1983 Four Arts Center, Institute of Contemporary Arts, Tallahassee, Florida

1982 Arab Heritage Gallery, Al-Khobar, Kingdom of Saudi Arabia

1981 Capricorn Galleries, Bethesda, Maryland

1979 Youngstown State University, Youngstown, Ohio
William Sawyer Gallery, San Francisco, California
Texas Tech University, Lubbock, Texas
Massillon Museum, Massillon, Ohio
San Jose Museum of Art, San Jose, California

1978 American Institute of Architects, San Francisco, California
Greater Birmingham Arts Alliance, Birmingham, Alabama
Chautauqua Art Galleries, Chautauqua, New York

1977 William Sawyer Gallery, San Francisco, California
University of Arkansas, Fayetteville, Arkansas

Group Exhibitions

1986 Gallery Henoch, New York, New York
North Miami Museum of Art,
North Miami, Florida
Hodgell Gillman Gallery, Tampa, Florida
Springfield Art Museum, Springfield,
Missouri

1985 The Tampa Museum, Tampa, Florida
Chautauqua Art Galleries, Chautauqua,
New York
Birmingham Museum of Art,
Birmingham, Alabama
The Deland Museum of Art, Deland, Florida
Anchorage Historical and Fine Arts Museum,
Anchorage, Alaska
West Bend Gallery of Fine Art,
West Bend, Wisconsin
Waterloo Art Center, Waterloo, Iowa
Ft. Wayne Museum of Art, Ft. Wayne, Indiana
W.C. Bradley Company, Columbus, Georgia
Valencia Community College, Orlando,
Florida
Foster Harmon Galleries of American Art,
Sarasota, Florida
Arkansas Arts Center, Little Rock, Arkansas
Alaska State Museum, Juneau, Alaska
North Texas State University, Denton, Texas
Springfield Art Museum, Springfield,
Missouri
Beaumont Art Museum, Beaumont, Texas
Florida State University, Tallahassee, Florida

1984 The Deland Museum, Deland, Florida
Equitable Gallery, New York, New York

1983 Washington and Jefferson College,
Washington, Pennsylvania
Provinceton Art Association, Provinceton,
Massachusetts
Abilene Fine Arts Museum, Abilene, Texas

Auburn University, Auburn, Alabama
Parthenon Galleries, Nashville, Tennessee
Arkansas Arts and Science Center, Pine Bluff, Arkansas
45th Annual Exhibition of Contemporary American Painting, Palm Beach, Florida

1981 Southeastern Center for Contemporary Art, Winston-Salem, North Carolina
Arkansas Arts Center, Little Rock, Arkansas
Birmingham Museum of Art, Birmingham, Alabama
Springfield Art Museum, Springfield, Missouri
Chautauqua Art Galleries, Chautauqua, New York
Henderson State University, Arkadelphia, Arkansas
Davenport Art Gallery, Davenport, Iowa

1979 Foothills Art Center, Golden, Colorado
Oakland Museum, Oakland, California
Butler Institute of American Art, Youngstown, Ohio
Sunne Savage Gallery, Boston, Massachusetts
Laguna Gloria Art Museum, Austin, Texas
Springfield Art Museum, Springfield, Missouri
Arkansas Arts Center, Little Rock, Arkansas
(continue to the next page)

Group Exhibitions
(continued)

1978 Chautauqua Art Galleries, Chautaugua, New York
Chapman College, Chapman, California
The Museum of Texas Tech University, Lubbock, Texas
Columbus Museum of Arts and Sciences, Columbus, Georgia
College of Marin, Kentfield, California
Fort Hays State University, Hays, Kansas
Scottsdale Center for the Arts, Scottsdale, Arizona
Birmingham Museum of Art, Birmingham, Alabama
Coos Art Museum, Coos Bay, Oregon
Arkansas Arts Center, Little Rock, Arkansas
Cheney Cowles Memorial Museum, Spokane, Washington

1977 San Francisco Museum of Modern Art, San Francisco, California
Pensacola Junior College, Pensacola, Florida
Springville Museum of Art, Springville, Utah
LaGrange College, LaGrange, Georgia
Laguna Gloria Art Museum, Austin, Texas
Washington and Jefferson College, Washington, Pennsylvania
Springfield Art Museum, Springfield, Missouri
Meadows Museum of Art, Shreveport, Louisiana
Chautauqua Art Galleries, Chautauqua, New York
Arkansas Arts Center, Little Rock, Arkansas
Oklahoma Museum of Art, Oklahoma City, Oklahoma
Fine Art Center, Sioux Falls, South Dakota

University of New Orleans,
New Orleans, Louisiana
Foothills Art Center, Golden, Colorado
Birmingham Museum of Art,
Birmingham, Alabama
Parthenon Galleries, Nashville, Tennessee

1976 Butler Institute of American Art,
Youngstown, Ohio
Cooperstown Fine Arts Center,
Cooperstown, New York
Laguna Gloria Art Museum, Austin, Texas
Foothills Art Museum, Golden, Colorado
Birmingham Museum of Art,
Birmingham, Alabama
George Walter Smith Art Museum,
Manchester, New Hampshire
Arkansas Arts Center, Little Rock, Arkansas Oklahoma
Museum of Art,
Oklahoma City, Oklahoma
Meadows Museum of Art,
Shreveport, Louisiana
Springfield Art Museum, Springfield, Missouri
Northern Illinois University, Dekalb, Illinois Georgia
Institute of Technology, Atlanta, Georgia
Hunter Museum, Chattanooga, Tennessee Montgomery
Museum of Fine Arts, Montgomery, Alabama
Chautauqua Art Galleries, Chautauqua, New York

Permanent Collections

Aerojet General, LaJolla, California
Arab Heritage Gallery, Al-Khobar, Kingdom of Saudi Arabia
Arkansas Arts Center, Little Rock, Arkansas
The Artery Association, Bethesda, Maryland
Arts and Science Center, Pine Bluff, Arkansas
Bank of Commerce, Tulsa, Oklahoma
Barnett Bank, Jacksonville and Tampa, Florida
Beaumont Art League, Beaumont, Texas
Birmingham Museum of Art, Birmingham, Alabama
W.C. Bradley Company, Columbus, Georgia
Butler Institute of American Art, Youngstown, Ohio
Carnegie Institute, Museum of Art, Pittsburgh, Pennsylvania
Chase Manhattan Bank, New York, New York
City Hall, Tallahassee, Florida
Crooker Bank, Los Angeles, California
Debevoise and Plimpton, Washington D.C.
Equity Life Assurance, New York, New York
Florida National Bank, Jacksonville, Florida
Fort Smith Art Center, Fort Smith, Arkansas
Hallmark Card Corporation, Kansas City, Missouri
Henderson State University, Arkadelphia, Arkansas
Hyatt Regency, Chicago, Illinois
IBM Corporation, Charlotte, North Carolina
Kaplan, McLaughlin, Diaz, San Francisco, California
Louisiana College, Alexandria Louisiana
McDonalds Corporation, Chicago, Illinois
Meadows Museum of Art, Shreveport, Louisiana
Metro-Dade Center, Miami, Florida
Mobile Oil, Houston, Texas
Nantucket Industries, New York, New York
Northwest Mutual Life, Milwaukee, Wisconsin
Parthenon Galleries, Nashville, Tennessee
Royal Commission, Jubail, Kingdom of Saudi Arabia
School of the Ozarks, Point Lookout, Missouri
Southern Bell Corporation, Miami, Florida
Springfield Art Museum, Springfield, Missouri
Sun Bank, Jacksonville, Florida
3M, St. Paul, Minnesota
University of Arkansas, Fayetteville, Arkansas
Western Electric, New York, New York

Opposite page
Title: *The Last Leaf*
Year: 1991
Medium: Watercolor
Size: 22" X 30"

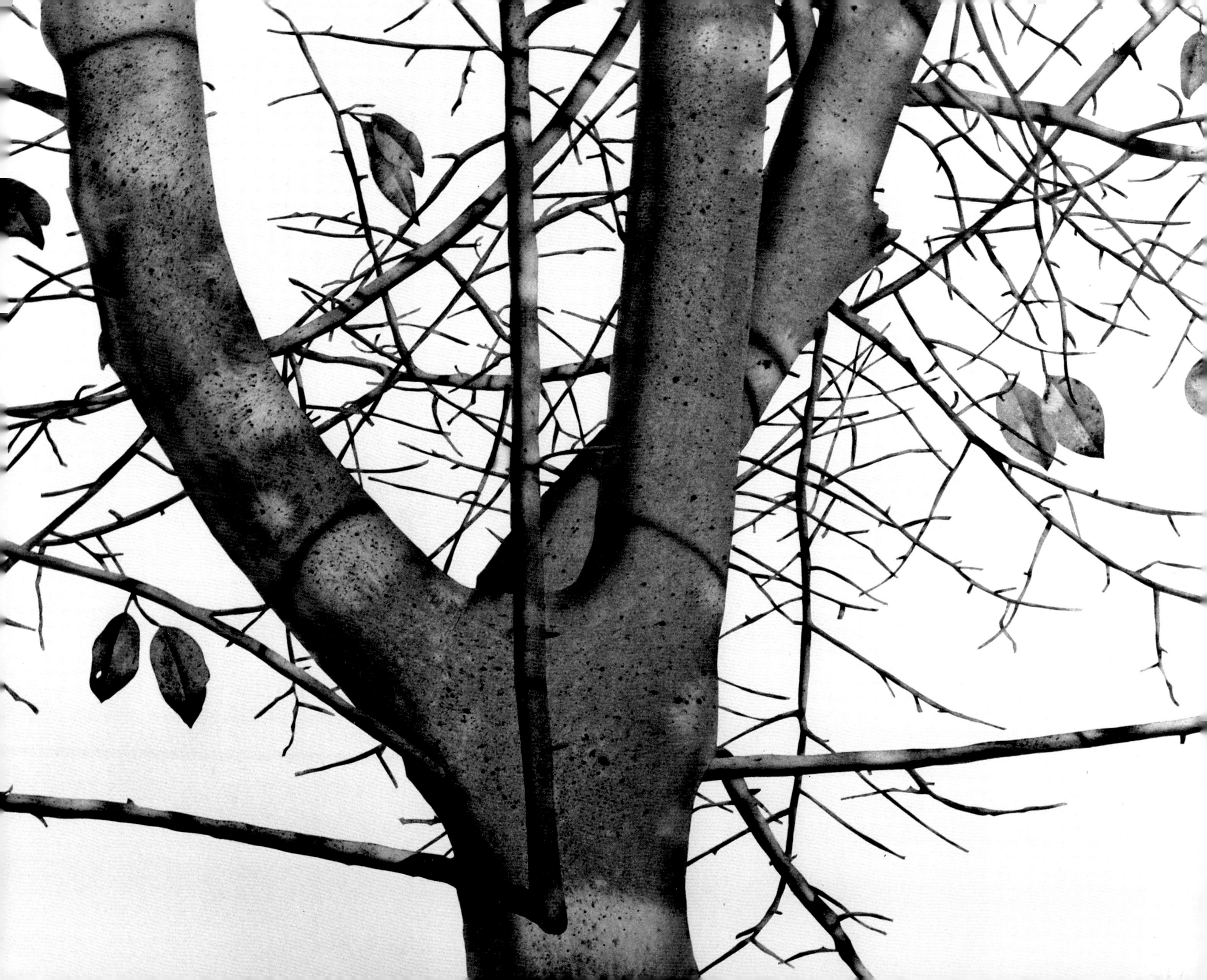

Notes

Narrative by Donald Harington

[1]Jean Grant, "Artist Presents Tension, Strength He Feels from Kingdom's Construction," *Arab News,* April 18, 1982.

[2]Letter to the author, from George Dombek, November 15, 1993, p. 14.

[3]George Dombek, "George Dombek Bio," typescript prepared for the author, September 23, 1993, p. 6.

[4]George Dombek, *An Investigation of the Development of My Work from March 1975 to October 1976,* A thesis submitted in partial fulfillment of the requirements for the degree of Master of Fine Arts, the University of Arkansas, 1977.

[5]pp. 10 - 11.

[6]Letter to the author, from George Dombek, December 8, 1993, p. 1.

[7]Letter to the author, from George Dombek, November 15, 1993, pp. 15 - 16.

[8]Betty Rogers Rubenstein, "Essay," *George Dombek Paintings 1975 - 1988* (Youngstown, Ohio, The Butler Institute of American Art, May 7 - June 6, 1988), p. 10.

[9]Ann W. Heymann, "George Dombek at William Sawyer, San Francisco," *Art Voices South,* January/February, 1980.

[10]"George Dombek Bio," p. 8.

[11]Letter, November 15, 1993, p. 6.

[12]Al Morch, "Fire Escapes Through An Artist's Eye," *San Francisco Examiner,* September 10, 1979, p. 27. Morch wrote of Dombek's San Francisco paintings, "His bold, super real excursions are so well executed that one would not be remiss in calling Dombek the master of the 'iron landscape.'"

[13]Louis Zona, "Interview with George Dombek," in *George Dombek Paintings 1975 - 1988,* p. 29.

[14]Zona, p. 23.

[15]Letter, November 15, 1993, p. 8.

Supported by the Ohio Arts Council, the Butler Institute issued the catalog, designed by Victoria Newcomb and printed in Tallahassee, Florida. In addition to the essay by Betty Rogers Rubenstein and the interview with Louis Zona, executive director of the Butler Institute, it contained a foreword by John Caldwell, curator of contemporary art at the Carnegie Museum of Art in Pittsburgh.

[16]Letter, November 15, 1993, p. 10.

[17]In his letter to the author of December 8, 1993, Dombek wrote, "You are correct in assuming that there are large areas which I believe the Chinese refer to as the 'happy accident.' Even though the paintings may appear highly controlled in their execution...I certainly have more affinity to the Dada movement than the Surrealist. It's somewhat of a contradiction but I often try *to plan chance*."

[18]Alfred Frankenstein, "A New Painting with Spirit," *San Francisco Chronicle,* December 19, 1977, p. 45. Writing of the fire escape series, the critic said, "Dombek's neutral colors and straight lines are often relieved by a puddling of pigment that counteracts their severity."

[19]Mark Hinson, "Italy's Isle of Elba Inspired Artist's Prolific Rocky Period," *Tallahassee Democrat,* March 28, 1993, p. 9F.

[20]Letter, November 15, 1993, p. 11.

[21]p. 12.

[22]p. 12.

Painting Index

P. 49, *Blue Grid*, 1986, watercolor, 30" x 42"

P. 50, *Inside the Barn*, 1987, watercolor, 40"x 60"

P. 51, *Barn*, 1987, watercolor, 40" x 60"

P. 52, *Lake Michigan Rocks*, 1994, watercolor, 30" x42"

P. 54, *White & Blue Rocks*, 1993, watercolor, 22" x 30"

P. 55, *Fish Creek*, 1994, watercolor, 22" x 30"

P. 56, *White Rock*, 1990, watercolor, 22" x 30"

P. 57, *Marble Rocks*, 1994, watercolor, 22" x 30"

P. 58, *Alberta*, 1994, watercolor, 22" x 30"

P. 59, *North Port*, 1993, watercolor, 22" x 30"

P. 60, *Rocks of Lake Michigan*, 1994, watercolor, 22" x 30"

P. 61, *Mulberry River*, 1994, watercolor, 22" x 30"

P. 62, *Seven Red Rocks*, 1994, watercolor, 30" x 42"

P. 63, *Turner's Bend*, 1994, watercolor, 22" x 30"

P. 64, *Gems*, 1993, watercolor, 30" x 42"

P. 65, *Rock Study #6*, 1994, watercolor, 8" x 8"

P. 65, *Rock Study #8*, 1994, watercolor, 8" x 8"

P. 66, *Red Rocks*, 1994, watercolor, 30" x 42"

P. 67, *Washington Island*, 1993, watercolor, 22" x 30"

P. 68, *The Placement of Rocks*, 1993, watercolor, 22" x 30"

P. 69, *Figure in the Rocks*, 1990, watercolor, 22" x 30"

P. 70, *Tour de Tree*, 1994, watercolor, 40" x 60"

P. 72, *Park in Florence*, 1989, watercolor, 22" x 30"

P. 73, *Tree Grid*, 1991, watercolor, 30" x 42"

P. 74, *Tree of Life*, 1988, watercolor, 40" x 60"

P. 75, *Tree Line*, 1991, watercolor, 30" x 42"

P. 76, *Red Heart Leaves*, 1994, watercolor, 22" x 30"

P. 77, *Dialog*, 1988, watercolor, 40" x 60"

P. 78, *Birch Tree*, 1990, watercolor, 40" x 60"

P. 79, *Golden Leaves*, 1994, watercolor, 22" x 30"

P. 80, *The Streets of Florence*, 1991, watercolor, 40" x 60"

P. 81, *Karen's Bike*, 1993, watercolor, 30" x 42"

P. 82, *Palazz Medici*, 1991, watercolor, 40" x 60"

P. 83, *Yellow Bicycle*, 1981, watercolor, 40" x 60"

P. 84, *Yellow Seat*, 1991, watercolor, 40" x 60"

P. 85, *Stick Bike*, 1994, watercolor, 30" x 42"

P. 86, *Top Flight*, 1994, watercolor, 30" x 42"

P. 87, *Touring*, 1994, watercolor, 30" x 42"

P. 90, *Barn 'X'*, 1987, watercolor, 30" x 42"

P. 97, *The Last Leaf*, 1991, watercolor, 22" x 30"